Consequences of a SideChick

Based on a True Story

A Novel By Vladimir Dubois

DEDICATION

Dedicated to three souls that were gone too quickly. "Bob" Luxaint, Roland Dorant, and Sandley Juste. You will forever be in our hearts.

ACKNOWLEDGMENTS

I want to take the time to acknowledge and thank all of those who have supported me and supported Consequences of a SideChick. I appreciate you all. To the cast members of Consequences of a SideChick: The Play 1&2, thank you for your hard work. I also want to thank Valerie Desir for your dedication and all that you do. And most importantly, I thank the Man upstairs for not giving up on a lost soul and blessing me with wonderful children, Vladius and Vera Dubois.

THINGS AREN'T ALWAYS WHAT THEY SEEM. A BEAUTIFUL FLOWER MAY HAVE AN AWFUL SMELL. IT'S USUALLY THE ODD THINGS THAT WE'RE NOT SEARCHING FOR THAT HAVE THE BETTER TASTE AND SMELL.

WHAT YOU'RE ABOUT TO READ IS BASED ON A TRUE STORY, MY STORY. IT'S A LESSON TO BOTH MEN AND WOMEN. JUST BECAUSE IT LOOKS GOOD, DOESN'T MEAN IT TASTES GOOD. MY LIFE HAS ALWAYS BEEN A STORY, BUT THIS HERE IS MORE LIKE A LIFE CHANGER.

Intro

"WHO I WAS TO WHO I AM"

Before I begin with my story, you must first know who I was to better understand why people couldn't believe all the events that you're about to read. Throughout middle and high school, I was known as Tyson. Nicknamed after one of the greatest heavy weight champions in boxing. I was given the name Tyson because I was always fighting. And when I fought, it usually ended up with my opponent knocked out. I was not your typical middle schooler. I weighed 230 pounds and was about 5 foot 8 inches. Throughout the middle and high school years, I maintained the reputation of being ruthless. I was the baddest and the strongest kid in my school. There weren't many other kids that were bench pressing 315 lbs. at the tender age of 16. Bold and stocky, I was making my way to the top of the food chain. As time passed, I became the most popular person in north Miami. I knew a lot more people because of my reputation. I had a large crew of people supporting me like a band of brothers, but I always kept a small circle of people I trusted around me. People from other schools would come to fight me and sometimes they would bring forty to fifty guys. I know it sounds unbelievable, but it's true. Trust me, they weren't there to bake cookies. Because of my popularity, other people felt that if they could beat me, they would be popular and feared. But I was too strong and my crew was stronger and better than theirs. I didn't care who I fought. I felt I had a purpose in life now. To defend my title and my territory, which was north Miami. If that meant I had to whoop on kids my age, girls, boys, and even adults, then I would. Anyone that wanted to challenge me, I took them on.

For the next couple of years, until I graduated high school, I ruled the school with an iron fist. No one thought I would ever be in a relationship, or even maintain a relationship because of my aggressiveness and reputation. I had to keep my image at a raw status. Only my closest friends knew me well, and those that didn't know me, feared me. If they didn't fear me, they respected me. People who knew me all wondered what happened to me after high school. Some people said I was in prison, some even said I was in the military. The truth is, I had moved out of Miami for a better life and ended up in the imperial Polk county, Florida. I lived in a very small town in the middle of nowhere. I ended up working for a prison as a guard. Security was my major. I went from this kid with a bad boy image to a man wanting to help people. I went to college, but I didn't finish. My whole life had changed. That kid that I was in high school was no longer me. I had a lot of responsibilities and bills to pay. I found out that there's consequences when you do wrong. I became an adult. I was a little bit calmer, laid back, a stay at home kind of guy. I spent eight years in Polk county after high school. A lot different than Miami, it was slow paced, but very affordable. Life was good, not great, but good.

CHAPTER ONE
"SWEET... THEN SOUR"

This is where my story begins, Polk county, Florida. There's not much to do here. But, it's a place where everything is a little bit cheaper, especially coming from Miami. This was where I met Francis. She was a nice, older, country girl. Not like other girls, more conservative. She was short and chunky, smiled from ear to ear, and wore thick glasses. She lived on her own and was very shy, but outgoing too. She was an independent woman. I was working at winter haven hospital as a security officer and she was working as a house keeper. We hit it off at the hospital while hardly working. We did more talking than work. We conversed about how country Polk county was. We laughed and enjoyed each other's company. One day, while we were working, I asked her out to the movies. She was very shy, and a little nervous, but said yes. From then on, we were in a relationship. Our relationship wasn't so bad, it was just plain.

I was content until I met her sister. A couple of years after Francis and I started dating, her sister came by her house to visit. Her name was Tay and I had never met her before. For some reason, she wasn't too fond of me from what I could tell. Me and Francis had moved in together and Tay didn't like it. She gave me the most hateful look a human being can give. From what I knew, Francis' mother had died, killed by a truck driver. Francis and Tay didn't get along because Tay felt that their mother favored Francis more. Tay was the second oldest out of four kids. She was 44 years old at the time. When she came over to the house that first time, she walked with a slow pace. Side to side like she was doing the cha cha slide. Her face looked greasy and her Sunday dress looked worn out. She was about 5'9" and weighed about 230lb. Tay was dark-skinned and had a face only a father could love. She made eye contact with me and cha cha slided my way.

The first thing she said to me was, "So you him?" in her country voice. I said, "Yup." with a little attitude. I knew that me saying "yup" like that, was going to start something, but I was ready. She became aggressive, gave me a lot of attitude. She said, "I don't know what my sister told you, but I love her more than you ever will." Huh? Where did that come from? Why did she say that to me? This was only the first time that I'd ever met her. Now my wall was up, my defenses on standby. I snapped back and said, "I doubt that!" Personally, I was confused. Why was this the first thing you say to someone you've just met? Now my first impression of her was that she was a bitch. Francis just stood there quiet near the door way, with nothing to say.

I thought Francis would've stood up for me, but she didn't. Her sister said with a serious face, "Let's pray. I'm a Christian woman and I wanna save ya souls (in her country voice)." She placed her right hand on my head and said, "Lord, let us pray for this devil." I pushed her hand off my head and said, "Is she serious?" with a smirk on my face. Although I was smirking, I was mad as hell! Did this bitch just call me the devil? I was looking at Francis hoping she would say something, stand up for me, but she remained quiet and unemotional. From then on, I realized that when it came to her family, Francis would let them run over me and that thought was embedded in my mind for years. Tay replied, "Your soul needs to be cleansed." I said to her, "How the hell the devil gonna pray for me?" She looked at the ceiling with her eyes rolling to the back of her head and said, "Lord, let me go before he cause me to lose my Christianity." She called out to Francis, "Walk me out lil sista," and she reached her hands out to her.

I told myself then, if Francis grab that bitch's hand, it would be over for me and her. With no hesitation, Francis grabbed her sister's hand and walked outside. I thought that was the most fucked up introduction ever. What really hurt was that Francis didn't defend me. Francis let me down when she took her sister's hand and walked outside. She didn't even see her sister's wrongdoing? It hurt, but now I knew where I stood with her. As I looked out the window, I saw them walking from the back yard to the front holding hands like they loved each other now. When her sister left and Francis came back in, we didn't talk for almost an hour. She finally asked "What's wrong?" I told her, "You didn't defend me." She walked off with a sadness, but I didn't care. After that, we weren't the same, or better yet, I wasn't the same. I didn't want to be with Francis after that situation with her sister. I generally did love Francis, so it wasn't that easy to just up and leave.

We were together several more years, then she wanted marriage. I could've given it to her easily. The love was there, but the certainty of our relationship wasn't. Is this what

I really wanted? She was a good woman for the most part, just old fashion. But honestly, not a strong individual. She wasn't strong enough to hold her own physically, but financially she could do for herself. I respected that. I could teach her a few things, but I was lazy and wasn't up for it. She cooked, cleaned, and really never argued about anything, not even about money. She was a catch. The "good girl". She wondered and asked, "Why don't you marry me?" I wanted to say, "I don't like your sister and I didn't like that you didn't defend me, " but instead, I used the excuse, "my money ain't right". After all this time, her not defending me from her sister still bothered me, but we never talked about it. I didn't want to marry a weak woman. She knew it was bullshit, but the crazy thing is, she stayed. I was sure she was going to leave me. Instead, she became quiet, and passive. Our relationship started to deteriorate. I knew I loved her, but I didn't want marriage yet. But the pressure was there.

About a year after I had met her sister, Tay, I finally got to meet her brother, berns. He was the oldest sibling and was a little bit different from Tay. He came by the house one day that Francis and I were both off. I told Francis I didn't want to meet him. I had a feeling he was going to be just like Tay or maybe worse. Francis begged me to meet her brother. I couldn't say no to her because she never asked me for much. As Francis allowed him in the house, I came out of the room to greet him. I extended my hand out and said to him, "hello." he was tall, stood about six feet, and had a lot of white hair on his chin. He shook my hand and said, " hey young man, how you doing?" with a country boy accent, a firm hand shake, and a military posture. I could tell that he was a man who liked to be in control. He told me to have a seat because he wanted to ask me some questions. Berns was treating me like a child in my own house, but I was still showing him respect. This was one of the reasons I didn't want to meet him in the first place. After several years of dating Francis, we finally meet. Two questions he asked me. "when are, you going to marry my baby sister? And "how much do you make?"

The tone of his voice was not pleasant. It went from pleasing to controlling. I was thrown off and in shock. I told him, "me and Francis are talking about marriage and I make enough to take care of me and her." he was upset. He wanted a straight forward answer. Without asking me for my name, he got straight to the point. The worse part was after all that, he still didn't know my name. What I really wanted to say was, "mind your Goddamn business!" once again, Francis stood by and watched as her sibling questioned me. I just wish she had a backbone to stand up against her siblings. I told him I had to use the bathroom, and I stayed in there until he left. I felt less attracted to a woman who didn't have a backbone. She was weak. Loud behind closed doors, but quiet in the presence of others. Damn, this was some bullshit her siblings were doing, and it was getting old.

Days and weeks went by. She could feel a sense of me pulling away. I loved her but hated her weakness. We didn't have any kids nor were we married, so I could leave as I pleased. I started going to the gym. It was a way to release my stress and enjoy what I love to do best which is weight lifting. Francis became clingy. She wanted to know my every whereabouts. We weren't intimate as we were before, but I wasn't cheating. I just needed time to myself. I was shaping up and she thought, "who is he shaping up for?" I started to think that she liked me fat and overweight because she never had an issue back then. One day, I actually said that to her. "you like me fat and sloppy huh?" she was so upset by what I said. But what does she expect me to think when she's mad that I'm working out? We were on a rocky road.

Francis had a niece named Netta. She talked to Netta about everything. I even found out that Francis was asking Netta for advice about our relationship. Somehow, her cell phone called me by accident one day. I could hear her asking Netta, "when a man says he needs some time, what the hell he mean by time?" When I heard that, I was like what the fuck?... I heard Netta talking about, "Girl, he either cheating or he making time to leave you." I was offended, I didn't like anyone in my business, especially her family members. And out of all people, why ask Netta for advice?"

Netta was going through some hard times with her husband that she had married when he was only 22 and she was 28. His name was tom. Tom already had kids from a previous relationship. Before Netta and tom were married, tom was in another relationship with a woman he left to be with Netta. To make it clear, he cheated on his previous girl with Netta. Netta went through hell to get tom. She finally got her man and even got him to marry her. Netta already had two kids from previous relationships as well. Netta was married once before, but got divorced. I thought, "how did Netta think tom was gonna be a faithful man, after what he did to the last chick?" the same way she got him is the same way she was going to lose him. After all the things Netta went through, she was the person Francis asked for advice? Netta was the wrong person to ask. Some men would consider Netta to be damaged goods after all she has gone through. When I saw Francis later that day, I didn't say anything about her phone calling me by accident. But then, I had to wonder, was it really by accident? Either way, I felt like our business was out there. And I wasn't happy about it.

I watched a movie and kept my mouth shut. She was

acting funny. Pouting and mumbling around the house. I didn't care, just laid down on the couch and turned the TV on to a movie. This went on for weeks. Netta called and told Francis she was pregnant with tom's baby one day. Damn, if she couldn't stand that man so bad, why she had a baby by him again? This was a funny situation. Talking shit about the man you with, but end up pregnant by him. Netta came over crying her eyes out. This, I had to hear. She was three and a half months pregnant, and tom wasn't working. Their situation seemed more and more dramatic. This was better than going to the movies. It was like watching days of our lives, but in 3d. Francis just comforted Netta and listened to her complaints of what tom did and what he wasn't 't doing. Shit, if I had to put my two cents in, I would've said, "Stop complaining and leave if he ain't doing right. It's your fault if you stay." that's what I wanted to say, but I was listening from afar in the bedroom and it wasn't any of my business. I wish I was sipping on some tea right now.

After Netta left, Francis said, "You love listening to drama." I replied, "Hell yea," and started laughing. Netta's situation wasn't funny but it was entertaining to listen to. Me and Francis was on talking terms again. Things seemed to be fine. Netta had her baby, it was a boy. Things were good between me and Francis for more than a few years after that. We had been together for a while now and Francis started to wonder, "after all this time, "Why haven't we been able to conceive?" At that point, I decided to go to the doctor to get my nuts checked.

When I went to the doctor, I had tests done on me. The results came in. The doctor said one side of my testicles was very low. I asked him what did that mean? He said, "At this point, it would be impossible for you to produce babies with the low sperm count." I was devastated but ok with it. I left the doctor's office and told Francis when I went home. That week, she bought fertility pills to help my nuts produce more sperm. I didn't care nor did I have faith anymore for producing children. I did what I do best, lift weights and I enjoyed doing it. I always see people who don't want children have them so easily and to me, that sucked. I know I could be a good father and Francis would make a wonderful mom. Whether I'm with her or not, she was one woman that I thought to myself would never put me on child support as long as I take care of my seed.

If I could get her pregnant I would, despite what we were going through. Almost a year had passed. Francis got up one morning as I was sleeping and was screaming with excitement. I jumped out of the bed screaming, "What's up, what happened?!" She was in the bathroom with a pregnancy test. She turned around and faced me and said, "I'm pregnant." the first thing I said was, "Who's the daddy?" Shit, doctor already told me I couldn't have kids, and I know Francis wasn't no hoe. If she was a hoe, I didn't know about it. I thought, if she was pregnant, then this was a blessing. I was just thinking of what that doctor told me. You know, doctors don't know everything. She was upset for the comment I'd made about who's the daddy, but I had to keep it real. Let me know up front. We decided to go to a real doctor, not just trust an answer from a stick. We went to a doctor who did a sonogram. I couldn't believe it, Francis really was pregnant. I was happy, but still in thought. A man can only wonder. I started buying things for the baby but didn't tell anyone yet until she was about eight months pregnant.

Time had passed and she was still upset about the comment I made. She said we didn't have to be together, just take care of your responsibility. I couldn't leave her now.

I wanted to see this baby. I slept in the living room, she slept in her room on her bed.

I finally told my closest friend, Mason. Mason was a man of logic. He would tell you what he thought and stick to his logic no matter what. I've known him since we were 5 or 6 years old. Mason told me about our high school reunion coming up in five weeks. I wasn't too eager to go. After all, I was bad as fuck in high school. I didn't want people talking shit about what I did to them back then. "Bitch, it was ten years ago, get over it." I told Mason I might go, but I felt like I probably wasn't. I had a newborn coming soon. Going to a high school reunion was the last thing on my mind.

CHAPTER TWO
"READING BETWEEN THE LINES"

I created a Facebook page that following week to stay in contact with family and friends I hadn't spoken to in years. I even made friends with strangers who I didn't know. At the time, me and Francis weren't at our best. I just thought we were done for the most part. I began exploring Facebook. Facebook was a site where you could be anything or anyone you wanted. Saw friends I hadn't seen or spoken to in years. I came across this one girl who's smile caught my attention. We became friends on Facebook. Her name was Trisha nelson. Our first conversation consisted of "How was your morning?" and "I like your pictures." From there, we continued to converse, but only on Facebook. Trisha had her information up on social media displaying her likes and dislikes. Specifically, she liked long walks on the beach and movies. It also showed that she had two kids and was a single mother. This information gave me the opportunity to get to know Trisha better, and as man, even use it to my advantage.

A couple days after conversing with Trisha, I called Mason and asked him about her. He asked, "You don't remember her?" I told him, "No, I've never seen her before but on her profile, it says she went to north Miami." He told me that's the girl all them boys ran a train on at red's house. I was shocked, "Where the hell was I when this was happening", I asked. Mason laughed. He told me it was more than thirty guys, and she knew what she was getting into because they told her before she walked in red's house. All jokes aside, I was like damn, I can't mess with this girl. Sure, I could try to fuck, but it wasn't worth it. When I looked at her pictures on Facebook, she had pictures of her in bikinis that showed her ass, and pictures of her sticking her tongue out at men. She seemed to be very sexual and provocative, but on her profile, it said that she was a Christian woman. Damn, the signs were there but I was just too curious.

I commented "sexy" on the bikini picture. Then I noticed this one guy that wasn't happy with her posting her picture up. I figured it was her brother because of the last name. He pleaded for her to take the pictures of her half naked body down in his comment. After hearing from Mason and seeing her pictures, I decided I'm not fucking with this chick. She sent me messages, I didn't respond. Over the week, she sent messages and flirting games on Facebook. I wasn't going to respond, but I did. Her messages said, "Where have you been" and that she liked me. I was flattered and started communicating with her again. A day later, she sent me a message that I thought was awkward. She stated, "Look, if you just trying to fuck, I'm not on that tip. I'm sorry if that's what you want, but that's not me." I responded with a question mark and asked her where is this coming from, because we didn't speak or mention sex in any of our conversations? I thought, this chick has issues. After my response, I got off of Facebook for the rest of the day.

That night, I checked my Facebook messages. I became a Facebook junky. When I looked at my messages, she wrote back. She apologized saying that a lot of guys hit on her only to try to fuck and she didn't know what I wanted. She inboxed me her phone number on Facebook. I was a little nervous to call at first, after all that I knew now, I didn't know what or where this was going, but I took a chance and called her. Trisha's voice sounded rough, like a woman who's been through a lot in her life. At one point in the conversation, she was yelling at someone in the background. It was day time. She was upset with her landlord who was upset with her for constantly paying late on the rent. This was the very first time I spoke to her on the phone, and she seemed like a rough neck. I asked her, "What's going on, are you alright?" showing my concern. She explained that her landlord was tripping about the rent, and she wasn't going to give it to him because the a.c unit wasn't working. She was aggravated and angered by the landlord. As we were talking, the father of her children came to her apartment to confront the landlord face to face. I thought, "What the fuck?" She assured me that her and her children's father had nothing going on. "He's just here to scare the landlord" she said.

I don't think Trish realized how this whole situation looked with her and her baby daddy. They seemed like they had a very friendly relationship, something like fuck buddies. I didn't care because I just wanted the same thing...that pussy. All this was going on while we were talking on the phone. I asked her, "Is your baby daddy there?" She replied, "Um, he's talking to the landlord about fixing the AC." Trish didn't really let me know when the baby daddy had left. I don't blame her because we weren't dating so it wasn't my concern. But, I felt it should've been common courtesy. She got upset and I wasn't sure why. I asked, "Trish, what's wrong?" She seemed agitated and frustrated, and told me her children's father did not talk to the landlord about the AC, but about him selling t-shirts. She called him a coward, and couldn't believe that he had tricked her into thinking he was going to talk to the landlord. I wondered, "How was she able to talk to her children's father if she's on the phone with me?" I figured, he either texted her or she texted the landlord. Either way, if she didn't want to tell me, I wasn't going to ask. I took her mind off that by talking about other things. I asked her where did she work? She said she was a teacher who taught people with disabilities for the city of Miami. I thought that was cool. She didn't ask me too many questions. She was more into herself. I didn't care, it was interesting listening to her. She had exciting stories that were entertaining. We talked for hours that first time.

It continued on like that, but each time I spoke to her on the phone she seemed to be tempered easily. Once, when she was driving and talking to me on the phone, she started cursing at another driver who cut in front of her. She went ballistic, but before she got mad, she said, "Lord, I'ma lose my Christianity if this bitch try me." I thought it was funny. Then, the same car that cut in front of her took the parking spot she was waiting to park in. She pulled up to the car and said, "Excuse me, you saw me waiting for that parking and you just took my spot". The person replied, "I don't see your name on it." Trish yelled, "Bitch, you saw me waiting!" The other person started yelling back at her. I heard the other driver say, "You ugly ass! Bitch, get your face fixed! Big nosed bitch!" Trish responded to the person, "Come fix my nose bitch, I'll mop the floor with yo fat ass." I loved it, it was exciting just to listen to all this on the phone. I might be dysfunctional to think this was exciting, but this was the most excitement I had in years. Better than watching television.

Trisha apologized to me. I told her it was ok, just calm down, don't let people take you out of your element. As she parked, I could hear her closing her car door and walking to the check cashing store as she said. She entered the door and the person who took her parking spot was exiting the store. Trisha said, "There goes that bitch. I wish you'd come fix my face bitch!" The person replied, "Bitch, you lucky I don't touch ugly." Trisha continued cursing until the other person left. When she got to the counter, she apologized to the clerk. I could hear the clerk say, "That's alright", but was laughing. Guess I wasn't the only one who thought this was funny.

I saw then that this woman had anger issues. I could read between the lines, but I just chose to ignore the signs. We spoke for a while on the phone that day. She was on her way to pick her kids up from daycare. She had two kids, a boy and a girl. Their names were Gina, who was two, and Justin, who was three. Justin was named after Trish's brother. Trish started telling me about the kids' father. Before she could get into her baby daddy's situation, she put me on hold. Trish said it was the cable man on the other line. She said the cable man was stopping by her home to set up her cable. I thought that was fishy. When she took me off hold, she continued her story about her baby daddy. She said her baby daddy was an alcoholic who cared about no one but his self. She didn't tell me his name yet. She was getting into more details of where he used to work before he became a loser (her words). She said he worked for the Miami herald making forty thousand dollars a year.

The Miami herald was laying people off, but they gave him a choice. Whether he wanted to be laid off or take a check for fifty thousand dollars? "He chose the check and spent it on friends and family, but not on his own kids that he had with me", she said. He only gave her a hundred dollars from that final check he received from the herald. You can tell by how she spoke, that she was bitter. But there was more that she seemed to be hiding. The details of who her baby daddy was as a man sounded more like a shark trying to rip open a floating pigs ball sack. She even spoke about her baby daddy's brother who was killed for being gay and trying to hook up with guys on the party line (better known as the chat line). His brother had life insurance. After he died, her baby daddy received the money to pay off his brother's house that his brother bought.

She told me so much about him. Shit, I knew everything about the man, even his birthday, which she later told me. Damn, I realize this chick can easily get someone robbed or killed with the information she was so willing to put out. As she was telling these stories to me, I listened carefully, but I felt that it was too early in our "phone relationship" to tell me these things. I mean, she didn't even know me well enough to tell me her deepest thoughts. I didn't know her long enough to tell her my deepest thoughts. She talked so much that every five minutes she would say hello just to make sure I was listening. And just so she knew I was listening, I'd ask questions like, "Why did you and baby daddy break up?" She responded saying that, "He cheated on me with a realtor who was the same age as him. He kicked me out of his house. And he even put a restraining order against me." Right there, that was a red flag for me. Then she said, "He didn't just kick me out, he kicked his own kids out as well." She paused and seemed to be crying. Telling me that she's had a hard life. This was beginning to be a little weird, but I still showed my concern.

I wanted to change the subject. I started talking about the high school reunion which was just weeks away. I told her I didn't think I was going but my boy Mason forced my hand. I wasn't excited for the reunion, but I told her that I definitely wanted to see her in person. She giggled a little bit. I was glad that I was able to get her mind off of what made her cry. I kept her laughing for as long as I could and made sure she was far from being sad and depressed again. Our conversation went on until she made it home.

CHAPTER THREE
"The High School Reunion"

Man! I was so fucking nervous when the day of the reunion finally came. People who weren't popular in high school, were popular now. The ugly ducklings became swans, and the nerds became gangsters. Damn, I see shit like this in movies. Me and Mason rode together in his car. I was wearing a black button down shirt, black dress pants, and black dress shoes. I was looking fresh, especially with my Versace shades. Mason had on all white but wasn't as fresh as I was. Before we even entered the building, there were a lot of classmates outside and they were surprised to see us. The place where they held the reunion was huge. It was at a hotel. Can't remember the name, not that I even care to know it.

I walked in and felt as if I was gliding through air. I saw old high school friends like Henry, Bo, and Red that I keep in contact with from time to time. There were girls who I had crushes on ever since middle school there. They were looking good enough to eat off a plate. Somebody was going to get pregnant tonight, I thought. Me and Mason arrived in the hotel. We walked into the banquette hall where they were holding the reunion. As soon as we walked in those doubles doors, it felt like all eyes were on us. Mason quickly found a table and sat down. I wanted a drink. Shit, they were serving free drinks, had to take advantage of that. While I was getting my drink, I saw Trish. She was a good-looking girl in person. Big lips, big nose, big eyes, and a fat ass. Call it what you want, but it was not a typical black butt. Naw, it was a fat black ass. I said, "Hey, what's up?" She answered me with one simple word. "Hey." I asked her a few questions but all her answers were either yes or no. Dang, all those times she would talk so much on the phone and now we're face to face and she's just giving one syllable words? She said, "I'm shy, a little nervous."

She was running around taking pics of a lot of people in the room. Didn't look shy to me. Music was playing and so I asked her, "Do you want to dance?" she said, "No, I'm too nervous ". I told her, "Ok, but before the night is over you will give me a dance." She laughed and said, "Ok, I'll be waiting." That was my cue. I told her that I would catch up with her later, just wanted to continue getting a drink. She walked off taking snap shots of everybody.

I then noticed a longtime friend, Julien, walk by Trish and squeeze her ass. She turned to see if I saw. I turned so she wouldn't know that I did see. Damn, what the hell did I just witness? A couple of minutes later, Julien walked up to me. He was wearing all white too. He had on a short sleeved white button down shirt. He left it halfway unbuttoned so the girls could see his chest. Nigga please! Julien gave me a hug and said, "I love you dawg. I ain't seen you in a minute." He reeked of alcohol. I wanted to ask if he was fucking Trish or was that his side chick. I didn't want to step on no toes. We were talking until other classmates started intruding.

Guess I was going to have to ask him later, but it was still on the back my mind the whole night. She wasn't my girl but like I said before, I wasn't going to step on no toes to make her mine.

The hostess of the reunion that night was Maria. I had known Maria since middle school. She was Red's girlfriend or ex girl at the time, too confusing. She had an announcement to make. She was giving out awards and playing memorial videos of those that had passed away. As the night got longer and the performer performed, it was finally time for a reunion picture. Everyone was laughing and having fun. We took several reunion pics, all of which I thought could've been better.

After the reunion, there was a club in the hotel and it was free to everyone there. I looked around for Trish but she was gone. Me, Mason, and a few other classmates headed to the club. When we got there, it was actually pretty nice. The bouncer let us in freely. I noticed an old classmate, Shantel. She looked good, but you can tell she was smoking that hard weed. The smell of weed was surrounding her. I said hi to her and she seemed not to even recognize me, so I walked off following Mason near the VIP area. Mason and a couple of classmates wanted to go in VIP, but no one had enough money to pay for it. I for sure wasn't going to pay a hundred dollars, got me fucked up! That's gas money for two weeks.

They decided to just hang out on the dance floor with everyone else. While I was on the dance floor, I saw Sheila and Andie on the dance floor. Ooooh shit! Just what the doctor ordered, chocolate and vanilla. Andie was a little too gangster and rough but very pretty though. Sheila was thick and nice and throwing it back at me. Wow, she got me. I was on it. Dancing with her definitely brought me back to that good ole Uncle Luke Saga. I was dancing with her for about thirty minutes to an hour. She walked off to get a drink and I couldn't wait for her to come back. I turned to my right and saw another classmate named Jen. Damn, she was the queen of gossip. Whatever she said, people somehow always believed her. And there she was, staring my way. No hi or nothing. It just looked like she was taking notes. No worries I guess. I'ma give her something to talk about.

As Sheila was coming back, I was feeling fresh and ready. As soon as Sheila got close to me, Trish jumped in front of her and started grinding her butt on my pelvic area. And yes, she was wearing a thong. Sheila stopped and walked off. I didn't see her on the dance floor anymore or for that whole rest of the night either. Trish was throwing her ass all over me and I enjoyed every moment of it. When I turned to my right, there was Jen once again staring with her mouth open in shock this time. All I could do was look directly at her and give her a thumbs up with a smirk on my face. She started laughing. "Yea, I know that caught your attention bitch." Trish's provocative dancing stirred up a lot of eyeballs our way. The night was pretty much over anyways. After Trish's provocative dirty dancing, she disappeared into the crowd. I then began walking around looking for Mason. I looked and saw Red hiding behind the DJ booth. Apparently, Maria was upset with him and was observing him on the dance floor.

The night seemed to almost come to an end. I finally found Mason. He was suggesting that we all head over to IHOP. I called up Trish and asked if she wanted to come along, but she said that's where she was already heading with Julie, another one of our former classmates. Julie was a friend. She was a heavyset woman who was known for the size of her breasts. I had known Julie since middle school also.

As Mason, Red, and a few other classmates got together, we all went outside. That's when I noticed Caleese aka Big Booty Caleese. She was well-shaped but had a booty that wasn't normal sized to the average girl. She was passing out a calendar of her half naked body to everyone as if she was a celebrity or something. I walked up to her to greet her and she passed me a calendar like I was a fan. "Oh hell naw bitch! No you didn't just try me like a groupie", I thought. I decided to walk off with a bad taste in my mouth. I threw the calendar away and we all headed to IHOP. We were in several different cars and when we got to IHOP, it was already packed with classmates.

Trish was there with Jean and Julie. I was surprised to see Jean there because I didn't see him at the reunion. I've known Jean since middle school. He was a cool friend but we never really hung out like that. They were all sitting at one table. I decided to sit next to Trish. More classmates started arriving. Then Julien, who earlier had grabbed Trish's ass, came in. He sat at the table where Red and Mason were sitting. Even Big Booty Caleese came. She sat where Mason and Red were sitting too.

I started talking to Trish. She seemed so shy. I knew I had to break that. I'd have to make her feel comfortable. I said a few jokes here and there to break the ice and it worked for a short while. She ordered grits and eggs with bacon. I got the pancake and steak. I enjoyed our conversation and I'm sure she did as well. I kept her laughing and blushing the whole night, so I know I was doing something right.

As everyone began to leave, it became apparent that some people were broke. They had no money to pay for their food. Julien ran to my table and whispered to me asking if I could pay for his food because he was "Going through some thangs", as he called it. My first thought was, "Nigga! How you payed for that gold around your neck?" But see, I knew him since elementary school and so gave him the benefit of the doubt and payed for his meal. When I was getting ready to pay, Big Booty Caleese walks by me and asked me to pay for her meal then walked off. "Bitch, you didn't even say my name right." I thought. So you know that wasn't happening.

I turned around and Trish was outside with Julie in a rented sports car. Mason and Red were walking out of IHOP. Maria was there too and I didn't even see her until I overheard her talking to someone behind me. When I got outside, I saw Julien talking to Trish. She saw me and began to move away from him as if she knew he was going to violate her in front of me or something. Julien turned and saw me walking in Trish's direction and said, "Thank you, homie. I love you dawg", and gave me a one-handed hug and walked away. I thought that was weird.

Trish seemed as if she had a lot of secrets. Damn, I started to get the feeling that it was a little bit more than I could handle. But we were just getting to know each other. I didn't want to know her dirty laundry, at least not yet. After Julien walked off, I asked Trish, "Is there anything going on between you two? Because I don't want to intrude." She said, "Hell no!" but her face told a different story. I really didn't want to get into it. Trish wasn't my girl and that wasn't my business. We talked about me leaving to go back to Central Florida the next day. I told her that I might need a ride to the train station. "The Silver Star train leaves at 12PM", I said. I suggested it to her and she jumped on the chance to take me. She smiled as if she had won the lottery. I thanked her and told her that I'd be calling her in the morning. I gave her a hug and walked to where Mason was.

Trish drove off with Julie in the car.

When I got to where Red and Mason were, Julien was there as well. He warned me. He said, "Homie, I see you trying to hit that, make sure you strap up with two gloves." I chuckled because it felt kinda awkward. Then Mason said, "Vee, you know that's the "manhoe" right? Don't get too attached." Red laughed, and told the story of what happened several years ago with Trish.

A while back, Trish and a friend skipped school and stopped by Red's house where there were more than 35 guys hanging out. Back then, Red's house was the hang out spot for the homies. One of the guys convinced Trish to come in and have sex with them. Trish's friend declined, but Trish accepted. Even after knowing how things were gonna play out, she still went through with it.

At the time, Trish wasn't on drugs nor was she forced to have sex with all these guys. When she walked into the bed room, condoms were being passed around to those who didn't have protection, just in case. Red explained how one by one, guys were losing their virginity to her. As I was listening to his story, I felt a little disgusted but sorry for Trish at the same time. She seemed to be a smart girl, but clearly lacked self-esteem. After hearing the story from red who was there from beginning to end, I didn't know what to think. I had heard this story from Mason before, but not in so much detail like Red's version. And I damn sure didn't know that the girl was Trish. Damn! I already told this girl to pick me up tomorrow, now I was having second thoughts. As I looked around, I noticed Julien had disappeared once again.

It seemed to be one of life's multiple choice questions. "Should I, A, continue messing with her and just try to fuck? Or B, move on and drop that hoe? I couldn't answer that question yet. I was curious and intrigued as well. I wanted to know more about Trish, but through her own words. I wanted to hear her side of the story. I took heed to the warnings Julien, Red, and Mason gave me. I decided to keep my eyes opened. At that point, everyone was going home. Mason dropped me off at my mom's house that night.

The next morning, I decided not to judge Trish of her past and see what she had to offer. I called her up early that morning. She said she was on her way to pick me up and I offered to take her to breakfast. She seemed so excited when she arrived at my mom's house. She was driving a gold colored Malibu. I grabbed my bag and placed it in the back seat of her car. First thing I noticed was her car was a bit filthy. Not to say I'm the cleanest person in the world, but there was food and trash piled up in her car. The only clean spot was the driver seat and that was only because she was sitting there.

She apologized for the mess and blamed her kids for it. It made me wonder, if this was the first time that you had me ride in your car, why wouldn't you have cleaned it before I got in? I mean, at least throw all that shit in the trunk or something. For her not to be bothered by it, it seems that she must've felt comfortable living in filth. But I wasn't tripping though. I was just hoping this is not how she really is. Maybe she was just too busy to clean up her car. So, I just squeezed myself in the car with the trash that was on the front passenger seat. Right before she drove off, I asked her, "Do you want to meet my mom? I just thought that was the respectful thing to do, especially coming from a Haitian background. Surprisingly, she said, "No, my hair isn't done and I look bad." Hold up, she was comfortable with me seeing her car being a mess, but she wasn't comfortable saying hello to my mom because her hair wasn't done?

I didn't have too much to talk about, just mostly about

how much fun we had at the reunion. We headed to a burger joint to kill time before the train came. She grabbed a table for us. I asked her what she wanted to eat. She didn't want much, just a number three on the breakfast menu. I, myself ordered a pancake meal. When I sat down with her, she was acting too shy to eat in front of me. She was taking little bites out of her food. Me, I was eating like I was at home with no problems. I even told her, "Don't be scared to eat in front of me, you good." She chuckled and smiled. That's when I realized her eyes were brown. I told her she had beautiful eyes. She said, "Thanks, I bought them." I laughed because I didn't realize that she was wearing contacts. Damn, she fooled me. She laughed too, no hard feelings.

We were done eating and went back in the car. As she was driving, Trish received a call from her co-worker, Keith. Trish put the phone on speaker. Keith told Trish that the people at work were mad at her for calling and saying that she was going to be late. She lied and told them that she had to take her kids to the doctor. Damn, I felt special. After she finished talking to Keith, I asked her, "Did you tell them you were going to be late because you wanted to take me to the train station?" She smiled and said, "Yes." I was a little blown away. Like damn, you did that for me? When we arrived at the train station, I grabbed my bags out of the car. She had a camera underneath the trash in her car. "Let's take a picture.", I suggested and she said agreed. We looked around and saw a heavyset young lady sitting down waiting for someone and asked her if she could take our picture. She said, "Yes." I grabbed Trish and pulled her close to me. She had her hand on my chest, close together. The picture came out great. Beautiful, if I do say so myself. She loved it so much, she put it as the wallpaper on her cell phone.

My train was arriving. I bent over to give Trish a kiss on

the cheek. She said, "No, not on the first day." I was like, "Huh?" I didn't want to complicate things so I gave her a hug and hopped on the train. I texted her, "Thank you for dropping me off." She said she enjoyed our morning breakfast. To me, this was the beginning of a beautiful relationship. I didn't want to tell anyone about me and Trish, especially after hearing what Mason, Red, and Julien had said. I just wanted to keep this on the low until we knew what we were doing. They weren't going to like me messing with Trish because of her background, but I wanted to get to know her for myself. I arrived home and all I could think about was Trish. She was a book and I was willing to read every page. I wasn't going to judge her from her past. As long as she don't bring it to the future, we were gonna be ok. I texted her, "Hey sunshine, I made it home." She replied, "I was so happy you asked me to take you to the train station, who am I? Smiles..." She seemed to have a way with pulling me in like a python. That whole day consisted of me and her texting back and forth. I wasn't going to tell anyone about how I was feeling about Trish because they would pass judgment on me and her immediately. It seemed like everything was going good. I made plans to see Trish again in a few weeks.

CHAPTER FOUR
"THE BIRTH OF A KING"

Weeks later, Francis and I began to communicate on good terms again. Francis didn't know about Trish, nor did she know I was even talking to someone else. She was pregnant and had only a few weeks left. I wanted to be there for my baby. I've never been a father so this was exciting for me. I hadn't told Trish about me expecting a child. I just thought it wasn't the right time to tell her yet, but to tell you the truth, I didn't really care to tell her.

I decided to take Francis to the park on a Sunday afternoon. She was a little stressed, and it wasn't because of bills. Even though things were somewhat rocky with Francis, I felt guilty. I felt guilty because I didn't tell her that I was seeing someone else. I was living a double life, but in some form of way, I was in denial about it. I hated the thought of me being seen as a bad person. She was pregnant and I didn't want to stress or upset her. Although we were in the same household, I slept on the couch. Whenever I spoke to Trish, it would be either when I was at work or when I got home. I respected Francis so I didn't do it in her face. I know that it didn't make it any better, but to me, Francis and I were over. We were unofficially broken up. To her, I was on a "time out" or "break". There was no mistaking it, I loved Francis, but we were too incompatible.

In my mind, I was constantly comparing Francis and Trish. Wishing that Francis was a little more like Trish in some sense. Trish was a woman who didn't take shit from people. I wish that Francis could be as aggressive as Trish. Sometimes, I almost wished that I could combine Francis and Trish and make them one. Trish, at the time, seemed more my type. Aggressive and more like a fighter. There was no doubt in my mind that I was stirring up a pot that was going to boil over, and when that moment happened, it was not going to be pretty. I guess you could say that I was somewhat confused. I lived in central Florida and Trish lived in South Florida. How was that going to work for me? For us? I wasn't going to leave my baby behind. I started having second thoughts. Like maybe I should stay with Francis and make the relationship work for the sake of our baby.

I have a father who was in my life part-time, but he was the best dad ever. I didn't want to be a part-time dad though. It was confusing, but I thought to myself, "let me ride it out." I went to every doctor visit that Francis had and every Lamaze class with her as well. The doubts that I had of the baby being mine, weren't there anymore. Being that I have never been a father before, I wanted to make sure that I would be the best father that I could be.

One day that week, I received a phone call from Trish. She was wondering why I hadn't called her in a while. My response to her was, "I've been working a lot of hours." She wanted to come see me in a few weeks. I told her sure. She had booked a hotel at the Ramada Inn for August 19th.

wanted to be in the delivery room with her sister, but at that point, I thought, "Who gives a fuck how she feels?" The doctor and I both walked back in the room and it was announced that only the father can be in the room with Francis. Tay gave me that look like she knew I had something to do with it. She mumbled something under her breath. I couldn't hear what she was saying, but I knew it was bad. Tay walked out of the room and told her kids to come with her.

It was three in the morning and I was tired. I sat there and watched Francis sleep for a long time. Seeing her lay in the bed, I thought to myself, "She's going to be a good mother." A little later, she asked me what I had told the doctor? I told her the truth. That I just wanted it to be me and her. Francis said, "I know you don't like my sister, but give her a chance and try not to let her get under your skin." I told her ok, and that I'd try. But I knew good and well it wasn't going to happen overnight.

My life was about to change forever. We started talking about names for the baby. She wanted to name him after me. I was happy, but I thought that instead of the exact name, let's try giving him a name that was different. A name that no one else had. The nurses came in and interrupted our conversation. They needed to induce Francis' labor so that the baby would come sooner. Francis was given shots in her spinal cord. Damn, it looked so painful. Her face showed a lot of pain but the nurse ensured her that everything was going to be fine.

It was getting a little late and I was hungry and tired. I left to go get a late-night snack. When I came back to the hospital, Francis went in labor again, but this time he was really coming. The doctor came in and checked on Francis.

For some reason, the baby was in the wrong spot and didn't want to move from that spot. Whatever was going on, he was still gonna come out today. The nurse burst the placenta so that the baby would move in a more appropriate spot. After all of that, the doctor decided that they would still have to perform a C-section on Francis. The baby was being too stubborn.

Francis was cut open while she was still awake, and I was watching the whole thing. Francis was singing while they cut her open. She sang, "God loves me" and in a brief instant, I had goosebumps. The song was beautiful and assuring. Finally, the doctor said to us, "he's here." They pulled him out and said, "It's a boy!" The doctor held him up, just like in the movie, the Lion King. Immediately, the song "The Circle of Life" started playing in my head.

Surprisingly, my baby didn't cry much. When they let Francis see him, she kissed him on the forehead, tears in her eyes. They asked me to cut the cord. My hands were shaking. I didn't want to cut the wrong thing off. The doctor held my hand and said I know how this must feel, but take a minute. I held my breath and cut the cord. I almost cried, but I didn't want my seed, my blood, my son, to see me cry. I want him to be a strong man. I want him to be a better man than me.

The nurse took the baby away to get cleaned up. She then asked me if I wanted to help clean him. I was scared to hold him, thinking I might break him by accident. She told me not to worry and gave me a sponge to clean off the blood. I noticed that my baby had a cone head. I asked, "Nurse, is his head going to be stuck like this?" She smiled. "No, it will get normal in a few days." As I held my son, I said, "I love you son. I will always be there when you need me." He opened his eyes and looked at me as if he understood. I felt a warmness come over me. The nurse came back and took my son.

Francis was then transferred to another room to recover after they sewed her stomach back up. I wanted to see my son again. I went to the new room where Francis was located. They brought my son in. Francis said to me, "I thought of a name." I asked her, "What is it?" She said, "You always said you were going to name your first son after your dad, but I wanted your first son to have your name. I've decided to give him both you and your dad's name. Maximus Deandre Dubois." I thought, "Wow, it has a ring to it." It was settled.

When the nurses brought my son, Maximus back to us, they asked if we had thought of a name yet. We said yes and told them Maximus. "Wow, that's Greek, isn't it?" I said, "Yes, yes it is. I thought of it myself." I felt a pillow hit me from the back. Francis said, "You thought of the name huh? That's alright." I said, "No, actually, we thought of the name together." I was happy. My baby boy was here. I began calling family members and telling them of the exciting news. As I was calling family members, Francis' sister, Tay, came in the room. She knocked and said, "God is good, where is my precious baby?"

She greeted Francis and didn't even acknowledge me. She walked up and saw my son, picked him up gently, and asked Francis, "What ya name him?" Francis answered, "Maximus." Tay asked again, "What you name him?" Francis repeated, "Maximus!" Tay said, "Lord Jesus, why you named him that?" I jumped in the conversation and said, "Because that's a strong name and I love it." She looked at me from the corner of her big eyes and sarcastically said, "I guess."

Francis looked at me and shook her head as a sign for me not to reply to her sister's negative comments. I told Francis I'd be back and went downstairs to the hospital cafeteria.

My phone started ringing, I answered it. It was Trish. She said she was in town and wanted to see me. Then she told me that her friends were throwing a party and she was going later to the party. I had completely forgotten that Trish was coming into town. I said, "Ok" and that I would come see her, but deep down, I knew that I was not going to go. Trish told me the name of the hotel that she was at as if she wanted me to come now. I did the only thing that I could think of doing at the time, I lied. I told her that I was at work at the moment. I really didn't plan on going to see her, especially on a day like today.

While talking to Trish, I get a text from my job letting me know that I can take a few weeks off of work to take care of my new son, but I would just need to sign some papers and pick up my check of the unpaid overtime that I hadn't been payed yet. At that moment, I started thinking to myself. "If I go to my job to sign the paperwork and pick up the check, I guess I could at least stop by and see Trish." I mean, we did already make plans.

Damn, in a way, I felt fucked up. Guilt was kicking in. I knew that if I went to see Trish, something was going to happen. After talking to Trish, I told her I would call her when I was on my way. Then she started sending me pictures of her booty and body shots. Man, I felt like I was being tested and I was going to fail the test with an F! As a matter of fact, an F plus for fucked up. I went back upstairs and Tay gave me a look like she was looking into my soul. "Why is this lady always trying me?", I thought. Francis was falling asleep and I was not leaving my son with Tay unsupervised. Shit, the bitch looked like a voodoo priestess. There was no way I was going to leave him with her.

Netta and her kids came upstairs to Francis' room. The room was packed now. I felt overly protective of Maximus. When Francis was free and able to watch him, I told her about my job wanting me to sign some papers, and that I would have to leave soon. I looked at Maximus and said, "I'll be back." When I left the hospital, I was excited that my son was here. It was truly the greatest day of my life. I headed to my place of employment, signed all the paperwork, and received my check. As I left the job, I received another call from Trish. I answered. She said that she really wanted to see me. I thought, not now, in my mind. But I said fuck it, her hotel wasn't that far from my job.

When I arrived at her hotel, it seemed kind of cheesy how the hotel was set up. No security, easy access, and it was in a bad area. I knocked on her room door and saw her slightly pull the window curtain and check to make sure it was me. Then she opened the door. She was looking really nice. I walked in the room and asked her how long was she staying. She said, "Only until tomorrow morning." I sat on her bed and said, "Damn, that's too bad." She said that she was going to a party with her friend tonight. I told her, "You must know the area well if you have friends here." She said she used to live here years ago.

Before I could say anything else, she hopped on me very sexually with her breast all in my face and her dress pulled up. I was thrown off mentally. I didn't see that coming. She started licking my earlobes, moaning, and getting me aroused. I wanted to stop, but I was weak. I knew if I came to see her, something was going to happen sexually. I couldn't stop myself. She started kissing my neck softly and gently. Her hands felt soft. As her lips came gliding across my chin, I could feel her breath on me. It was warm with a scent of fresh gum.

She took off her dress and ripped off my shirt. She pushed me down on the bed. She was aggressive most definitely. She got up and pulled my pants off like it was a magic trick. Hell, it usually takes me 35 seconds or more to pull my pants off. She did it in a blink of an eye. Then, she hopped back on top of me. I was getting extremely aroused. She began licking my chest and then moved her hands down, caressing my dick and then stroking it. I thought to myself, does Trish have a condom? I didn't say anything or ask for one, although I knew that I should have. Shit, I didn't know if Trish had any diseases nor did she know anything about me.

My body felt like it was being taken over and I had no control. I have never felt like this before, and believe me, I am far from a virgin. Her tongue was warm as she licked me from my chest to my belly button. She began twirling her tongue in my belly button, like a snake sticking it's tongue out. Her eyes opened wide. My mouth was watering. She grabbed my penis and sat on it, penetrating her vagina with it. "Oh my God, what am I doing?" I thought. No condom and no other protection, but it felt so good. I've never done anything like this before, but the crazy thing is that at this moment, I can't stop myself. What was wrong, felt so right.

The warmness of her wet juices began to flow down between my thighs. This was a dangerous game I was playing. She began using the muscles in her vagina to grab tight onto my penis. It felt so good. It felt like bliss. She's on top of me now, riding me like she was riding the sun. She starts screaming and moaning. I grab her waist and she pulls me where our chests are now rubbing against each other. Her moans get louder and she screams "I'm coming, ooooh my goodddd!!" We rolled off the bed and we both came at the same time.

We landed on the floor. She looks at me in my eye, her breathing heavy. I was breathing hard too. Damn, that pussy was good, but now I worried about what I'd done. I had unprotected sex with Trish the first time I laid in bed with her. We both were stretched out on the floor for a few minutes. She rolled over and laid her arms across my chest. I kind of felt weird. Here is a woman who could be sexually active. She's probably had a lot of partners and here I am having unprotected sex with her. It was funny that for her, having sex without protection, was not an issue. At least that's how it seemed at the time. She seemed more concerned about whether or not we were in a relationship now that we had had sex.

I could tell she was thinking that, even though she didn't say it. I got up, cleaned up, and told her I had to leave. She asked where I was going. I could tell that she wanted me to stay longer. I told her I was going to work, and to change the subject, I asked her about the party she was going to. I told her, "Maybe, if you don't go to the party, I'll come back and stay with you for the night." She looked like she wanted to say something. Her face looked confused. I put on my clothes and headed out the door like a hit and run car accident.

Trish started texting me, telling me she missed me. I didn't respond because the guilt was settling in hard on my conscience. Even though me and Francis had our problems, I know that I just did the unthinkable. How could I have been so weak? I knew what I was going over there for. There was no excuse, I thought. I fucked up. Damn, I'm so fucking weak! The human flesh is a sinful thing. I can't lie, Trish's sex style was a bit hypnotizing. More lustful than any other that I've come across. I've never dealt with a woman who can produce so much wetness. It caught my attention mentally. I had to have more of her, but I also needed to get checked. To tell you the truth, I was worried but I told myself, we all die someday. With that careless mind frame, I wasn't so worried anymore. But I knew I still had to get checked.

CHAPTER FIVE
"MY GUILT"

I made it back to the hospital around 6:30 in the evening. When I got upstairs, Francis was sleeping and Maximus was in his hospital bed. I grabbed a chair and moved next to Maximus' bed. I couldn't stop looking at him. I fell asleep as I was sitting down next to Maximus. When I awoke the next morning, Francis and Maximus were gone. What I had done with Trish felt like a dream. My phone started ringing, it was Trish. I first looked around to make sure no one was here before I answered it. She was calling to tell me that she was leaving and on her way back to Miami.

I was tired as hell. She wanted to have a conversation and I wanted to rest. She started telling me about how she had a great time with me yesterday. I asked her how the party was? She said, "It was ok." It seemed like she didn't want to talk about it. I told her I was going to call her in a bit because I had just woken up. She said, "ok", with a sadness in her voice. After talking to Trish, I got up and walked around the hospital until I found Francis and Maximus.

Francis was breast feeding him at the time.

Everyone in the hospital loved Francis. They accommodated us very well. They even let us stay for an extra day. The hospital workers told us not to worry about it and that the extra charge would not be coming out of our pockets. They also gave us free food and drinks and brought Francis flowers as well as gift baskets. We ended up staying at the hospital for almost a week. It actually felt like a long stay at a hotel.

The day came for us to take Maximus home. I can't lie, it was scary for me. He was a newborn and I didn't want him getting sick or anything else happening to him. Francis was off work for three months and I returned to work after a month. Trish was calling and texting me every day. Even when I told her I would call her back, she continued to text uncontrollably. She was sending me pictures. She was constantly texting me and asking me when we would be able to hang out again. That should've been a red flag for me, but I wanted to hit that pussy at least one more time. I finally told her, "Whenever she was ready." Almost immediately, Trish made plans for another trip to come see me.

While at work, Francis called me. She was stressing and telling me that she was a new mother and needed me to help her. I knew that for most new mothers, they experienced post-partum depression so I wanted to make sure Francis wasn't going to go through that. I told her that if she ever felt alone and overwhelmed, she needed to call me no matter what and I meant it. Post-partum depression is nothing to play with.

Trish texted me that she was coming next month on a Saturday. Damn, but I work Saturday. Fuck it, no problem, I would just switch with another person at work. Mason called me to congratulate me on the newborn. He asked if I had heard anything from the "Manhoe", which is the nickname that most people knew Trish as. I felt a little awkward when he said that, "but should I be?", I thought. I started thinking and hoping that I didn't catch any feelings for this girl. I'm still not sure of her agenda yet. I didn't wanna lie, so I told him, "Yea, I spoke with her. She even came to see me." "What the fuck? What happened? Don't tell me you fucked."

I told him the truth, "Yes, I did.", but I didn't tell him it was without a condom. He never asked, so I didn't say anything. He was in shock! "Vee, don't wife that hoe! Do you know where that hoe has been? I'm warning you brother, she will ruin your life. Heed my warning." I listened to every word that he said. But I was curious. I couldn't help but to ask, "What do you mean she will ruin my life?" Mason responded to me saying, "She's known to be a pathological liar. Not only that, she will put your business out there." As I reflected, Trish did seem a little unstable to me that first time I spoke to her on the phone.

Mason's warning seemed to be sincere. I told him, "Ok, I'll take your advice." He said, "No, no you won't. I know you Vee. Whatever problem you and Francis may have, try to fix it. If it's not what you want, then leave, but still take care of your son. But whatever you do brother, don't wife the manhoe!" Mason knew Francis. They'd met a year or so after me and Francis started dating. He knew that Francis was a good girl and he wanted to make sure that I didn't mess things up.

I told him, "Ok, but let's keep this between us." He said that he would, but told me, "Remember what I told you." I can't lie, his warning sent chills to my body, but like always, I never listened to Mason. I wanted to see the "manhoe" for myself. As time passed, I was still there for Francis. She was a good woman, but I really felt that we were too different from each other. Trish was calling me all the time and telling me how much she missed me. I kept thinking to myself that I need to get a blood test after our first encounter last month. Unprotected sex with Trish, what was I thinking? Honestly, I was scared to even know, but I had to find out if I was alright.

This was an uncomfortable conversation that I didn't want to bring up to Trish, but it was a must that we talk about it. I figured that the next time I saw her in person, I would talk to her about it. I checked my Facebook inbox and I noticed that I had messages from Trish. She was at work, driving her clients to their houses. I had forgotten that she drove mentally challenged people to their homes. At least that's what I got from what she last told me.

She was excited and making plans to come see me again. I was still thinking about what Mason had told me though. It was in the back of my mind always but like I said before, I wanted to see for myself exactly what this girl was all about. I was no prince myself, so I decided that I wasn't going to judge her. Me and Trish talked about the hotel and where we were going to go once she came. I promised her dinner and a walk in the park. She teared up and said that no one had ever done those things for her. I joked with her and said, "Listen, right now, we're just talking about it, it hasn't happened yet." She laughed and said it's the thought that counts. I let her know that I make promises and I keep them. She laughed again, and said, "Ok." The plan was set. Me and Trish were getting a hotel and Trish went ahead and payed for it. A couple of days later, she sent me the confirmation number for the hotel reservation.

Francis was taking care of our newborn. She was really focused now. It had been about a month since she came out of the hospital, yet she still wasn't one hundred percent herself. I felt so guilty. I went out of my way and made sure that Francis had everything she needed for Maximus.

The week came where me and Trish were going to meet at the hotel. This time, the hotel was in Orlando, Florida. It wasn't too far from my job and it was close to a lot of restaurants. I told Francis that I was heading to work early and to call or text me if she needed anything. She seemed emotionally uneven and looked at me as if she knew I was going to meet someone. I guess she had that women's intuition. I left early morning to meet up with Trish. Trish texted me the information of the hotel. I decided that before I get to the hotel, I would grab her some candy, liquor, and flowers. Just a little something to butter her up.

When I got to the hotel room, she was there waiting on me. She answered the door wearing a red thong and black bra. I was aroused before I could even come in. My dick was so hard that if I had turned around, someone's eyes were going to get poked the fuck out, seriously. She pushed me towards the bed, pulled off my shirt, and started licking my chest. Her body smelled like peaches from Victoria's Secret and that was a huge turn on.

She got straight to seducing me, more like sexing me. No kissing or hugging. Her breath had a scent that smelled like burning hair from a hot curling iron. I couldn't kiss her. Her breath was a turn off, but her body was a turn on, all the way on. She pulled off my pants and sucked on my belly button, then licked it. She slowly started making her way towards my penis. Her tongue felt warm. I was once again under a spell and I liked it.

She put her lips around my penis and engulfed it. It felt like bliss. Wow, this couldn't be her first time giving head, because she was very good at this. She had spit on the tip of my penis, this felt like a porno. Slobbering noises mixed with moaning was a turn on, to the point I was about to come. I didn't want to come too fast but her head game was a killer. I warned her I was coming. She just kept on going until I came and she drank my semen. I was sure that wasn't her first-time swallowing semen the way she did that. After she had swallowed the last drop, she lifted her head making eye contact with me and licked her fingers as if she was trying not to waste a drop of cum.

I gotta admit, that was the deal breaker for me. She had me at "yummy." I never had a woman that was so vulgar and proud of it. She laid back with her legs open thinking I was going to eat her pussy. "Oh, no way!" I wasn't going to return the favor. When I looked between her legs, she had an extra meat that was hanging from her pussy. It looked like something out of the norm. Like a kid growing up with six fingers, she had an extra skin on her vagina. I never seen that before. Was that going to stop me from having sex with her? Nope, not at all.

I thought to ask for a condom, but I wasn't thinking. Just horny, and ready to get it in. Once she opened her legs, my dick went right in. I could tell she was disappointed. She was waiting for me to eat her pussy, yet I was thinking, "Why didn't I use a condom...again?" Her pussy was warm and wet, just the way I liked it. I was moving in slow motion, listening to her sounds of moaning. After thirty minutes, I finally climaxed. When I was done climaxing, I looked at her. She looked at me, as if I was a science project watching me climax. We both laid on our backs next to each other. She rolled over and said she really liked me and asked if I could be her baby daddy. I pretended to act as if I was sleeping, snoring loud enough to tune her out. She wanted me to be her baby daddy? I thought she was   crazy. After an hour, I got up. Ready to eat, not pussy, but real food.

CHAPTER SIX
"THE HATERS"

I asked her where she wanted to go? She chose Chili's. They had a two for one deal. We both got dressed. As I watched her get dressed, I saw how her booty just jiggled. I was ready for round two, but we had to go. We left the hotel in my car. When we got to Chili's, we sat down and ordered lunch. We talked about ourselves, like what our likes and dislikes were and what she expected from a man and what I expected from a woman. She spoke about all her past relationships and how she was a victim of abuse, both physical and sexual. She even claimed that her oldest brother molested her. As she spoke, I felt sorry for her, she really seemed sincere. To be honest, I didn't think that conversation about sexual abuse was relevant at the lunch table. I did show some concern though, but this conversation needed to be changed.

I tried to change the subject by talking about the high school reunion. I told her how good she looked that night. It took a lot, but finally, she had a smile on her face. I didn't think anything could ruin our lunch, until she decided to tell me about Jen and Maria. She said that some of the girls told her that I wasn't serious when it came to relationships. I was blown away with that information. Whether it was true or not, these chicks needed to stay out of my business. I wanted to know who was spreading those kinds of rumors about me. When I asked her who told her, she didn't hesitate to tell me that it was Jen. Why would Jen say that? I was angry. What could be the purpose of Jen telling Trish that? Then Trish explained, it wasn't just Jen, but Maria too. Trish said, at first Maria was all for us hooking up until Jen got in her ears. Trish asked Maria a while back about me. Maria gave me some good compliments. Then Jen called her. After Maria and Jen spoke, Maria came back with a different attitude, telling Trish, "I don't think he's good for you."

Jen was a very manipulating bitch to me. Whatever she said, her followers followed. Sad to say, Maria seemed to be one of her followers too. She was also very gullible as well. She was trying to fit in with the wrong crowd of back stabbing girls who really didn't like each other, but could only stand each other for short periods of time. There was no loyalty between the group of girls that Jen was associated with. Secrets between those girls was like playing the telephone game. It never came back the way you heard it. I then realized why Jen would say such things about me. When Trish said Jen told her that I used to date her friend, I put two and two together. The only friend of Jen's I'd ever dated was Sheila.

Sheila was a cute girl. She was dark skinned, with short black hair. She had a gonzo nose, was a little on the plus-size, and a personality to match her stuck up attitude. She had always told me that she was a virgin. I guess I was her

49

first. Me and Sheila had dated on and off for almost two years. She had given me a choice to stop associating myself with Red, who was into Masonry. She had her own opinion about the Masons and said they worshiped the devil. She even went as far as sending me books and pamphlets about Masonry. I didn't want to hear it nor read it. Red was a long-time friend and was family to me. Although I had loved Sheila, she gave me a choice to stop associating with him, and so I chose to stop associating with her.

She was a controlling woman and that, to me, was a turn off. Leaving her wasn't easy but I had already seen that it was getting bad between us anyways. She felt since she made more money than me, she could control me, and that wasn't the case. I'm a survivor. She must have missed that part. I believe Sheila told Jen things about our relationship and Jen made it her business to expose it. Was Sheila that mad at me that she decided to tell Jen about our intimate moments?

The last time she contacted me was via an email. The first thing she said was, "I see you like playing games. I'm tired of you trying me." When I saw that email, I said to myself, "After all this time, why is she contacting me now?" We stopped talking years ago, I didn't know who she was fucking, but I wanted no part of it. I emailed her back telling her that I had moved on and so should she. I guess it hit a nerve because she emailed me back differently this time. The tone was like she was writing to cancel a reservation or something. She congratulated me, but you could tell that she was hurt. I hated doing that, but I had moved on. Sheila deserved someone who could put up with her shit, and I wasn't it. A year and a half later, I find out she had gotten married. What a coincidence. We never spoke again after the email.

After all those years, it felt like she came to hate on me. Why was me hooking up with anyone relevant to her or to Jen? Jen went as far as telling Trish, "You know everyone knows about your past. He's just probably trying to get what he missed out on." I thought to myself, what a fuckin hater. She thought she was helping Trish, but really this was hurting Trish mentally. Jen thought she was being a friend, but became a parasite instead. To be honest, I really didn't like Jen, but I respected her. This information I received changed the respect to despising her. From what I heard, she needed to worry about her husband, Mister Trick Daddy, is what the ladies called him.

The information Trish relayed to me was her way of wanting to know if I was going to leave her high and dry after a couple of fucks. If she'd believed what Jen had told her, I don't think she would have slept with me so easily, maybe she still would've. I asked her what were her thoughts about me. She said that I am a good-looking guy, different from the one's she had dated in the past. I asked her, "Why you say that?" She responded, "Because you seem to care." I asked, "So what your friends said about me, does it bother you?" She was honest and replied that yes it did bother her because she genuinely likes me and she already knew or heard me and Sheila had dated in the past. Now she realized Sheila and Jen were best friends. She figured something must have happened between me and Sheila, and Sheila was using Jen's manipulating tongue to damage my reputation.

I don't think the rumors really mattered to her, because Trish wouldn't have had sex with me, especially without a condom. Right? Anyways, after lunch, we headed back to the hotel. Trish received a call from the father of her children. While talking to him on the phone, she walked further and further away from me to talk to him privately. When she did that, I began to think that she had something to hide. While Trish was with me here in Orlando, the father of her children was watching the kids. I couldn't hear the conversation. She was trying not to say to many words. I guess so I wouldn't understand. I could only hear him asking her questions like, "Is your dad ok?" Hmmm. She didn't tell him where she was going, who she was seeing, or if she had moved on. I didn't think it was my business, so I didn't say anything and waited until she was done.

We had more passionate sex when we got back to our hotel room. We did it I think four times that day. Damn! I never did it that much in one day. I thought about what Trish said at lunch, what those haters had said about me. I'm not the type of guy to not want a relationship. It bothered me so much so that I called up Red and told him that his girl, Maria, was interfering in my relationship. Red asked, "So, are you messing with the manhoe?" It was an embarrassing question, but I never lied to Red before, so I told him the truth. "Yes." You could hear it in his voice like he was disappointed, but Red always stood by my side, whether I made good decisions or bad ones.

Red said, "I hope you don't fight me for calling her the manhoe." We always joked around since we were kids, so I didn't take what he said to heart. He just said, "If you like her, then I'ma respect that, but just know what you getting into. I'll talk to Maria to stay out your business." I thanked him. If Trish knew I spoke to Red about what she told me, she would be upset. I was getting tired of the hating though, and I could see how Trish felt at this point. It was almost like when people would say things about her being a hoe, at least from a man's point of view. Whether she knew it or not, I understood how she felt now. The girls talked bad about me and the guys talked bad about her. The next morning, Trish was packing up to go home. We ate breakfast and made plans to see each other again the next following month.

CHAPTER SEVEN
"A FRIEND INDEED"

While at work, Trish would always call me. By this time, we had been messing with each other for several months. She had no girlfriend title yet and I had no boyfriend title yet. I was fine with that, as long as I was fucking Trish. It's sad to say, but it's the truth. Yea, I liked her, but if she didn't ask, I wasn't going to say anything. After work, I'd go home. Francis would go to work. I'd check on Maximus to make sure he was sleeping then go on Facebook. I saw Trish on Facebook flirting with me on my status where everyone could see. She even went as far as saying things like, "I'm trying to see what's good with you boo." People would comment and say stuff like, "She's waiting on you dawg."

She wanted to publicize us on social media. Asking me on Facebook, "Are we together?" I had to call her because I hate posting my business on social media. I don't even put my real name on social media, why the hell would I put my business? Trish was trippin'. When I called her, she said she didn't think nothing of it. She was turning the situation around on me and seemed a little upset. She felt like I was hiding her. She kept asking, "Are we an item or not?" Finally, I told her, "What do you think?" Only to see what she would say, and her response was, "Yea, we are a couple." I said, "Well, then we a couple." After saying that, she calmed down. I saw right then that she could be very confrontational, but damn that shit turned me on. Seeing that a woman wanted me that bad is priceless.

Now we were together officially. Trish was happy as fuck. She couldn't wait to tell everyone she knew that she was in a relationship. The next day, the news was everywhere about me and Trish dating. A female friend of mine, Sherline, who I've known since childhood, emailed me on Facebook saying, "Hey, your girl over here telling people how ya made intimate love at a hotel. Put ya girl on check bro." I didn't know how I was going to approach Trish about her telling people of our sex life. Maybe I should just leave it alone, I thought. More and more people were emailing me on Facebook. Mason even called me and said he heard me and Trish were dating and people are talking about it. He said I don't know if you know this, but she likes attention. I told him, "I see. She seems like an attention seeker."

Mason informed me that she is advertising our relationship to everyone and asked me to just tell her to chill. When I hung up with him, I called Trish. She said, "Hey shou booboo." I asked, "What is a shou booboo?" She replied, "Something she came up with." I asked her straight up, "Trish are you telling people about us?" She said, "No." "Trish, I believe you, but if you are telling people, don't." She says to me, "If you believed me, then you wouldn't have said that." I told her, "I believe you." But I really didn't. She then got upset and said, "Well, since we on that subject, Anny said you tried to talk to her and that you said she can have your baby." Oooh my God! I was silenced for four long ass

55

seconds. I was surprised, ambushed. I asked her, "What are you talking about?" Then it hit me.

Anny was a high school class clown. She was short, stumpy, and a little overweight. Me and Anny was always cool, but as friends though. A while back, Anny was going through a situation where she felt she couldn't have babies. As a joke, I told her I wouldn't mind giving her some sperm. This was way before me and Trish made it official between us. Somehow, Anny got in contact with Trish and told her that. I told Trish, "Yea, I did tell her that, but that was way before we made it official." Trish said, "Why you on her Facebook page liking her pictures and telling her friend ya had a good time?" Wow, this girl (Trish) was becoming a headache.

Before I could say anything, she said, "I don't think this is gonna work out between us." I told her, "That's fine." And before I could hang it up, she screamed and started crying on the phone. "Wait, wait, wait please, I'm sorry. I didn't mean it like that. Please don't go, let's talk about this." She was in heavy tears. I thought it was over until she started crying loud again. I never had no one cry over me, begging me to stay. What a confusing situation. I told her, "Ok, let's talk about it." She kept apologizing. As easy as it was for her to apologize, it was just as easy for me to accept it. I told her that it was ok. She said she wanted to see me, so we made plans to see each other again. Later, I went on Facebook and deleted Anny from my page. I just didn't want any problems. I thought by deleting Anny, it would make Trish happy, but it did just the opposite.

A week later, Anny contacted me through Facebook email. She said, "Vee, I known you for a long ass time, and I'm about to reveal some things to you. Take it how you want, but just hear me out." I coulda easily deleted her message, but I thought, let me see what she had to tell me. I began reading her email. It said, "I just want you to know how Trish was telling people that you and her had sex. She said that she thinks she's pregnant and she's telling everyone she's in love with you. Vee, let me tell you, she's not the girl you think she is. She was homeless, staying at a shelter with her kids. She asked me if she can stay with me and even though I don't like people staying with me. I felt sorry for her and her kids. I told her she could move in, one of the worst mistakes I've ever made. Vee, I swear to you, she is a filthy woman who cleans her hair and panties in my kitchen sink. She will wear the same weave over nine months. Her kids are so bad. They peed everywhere in my house. Also, did she tell you she got into a fight at the shelter? She started the fight with another girl who was a little younger than her. The girl punched her in the nose. They fought in the bathroom stall. The girl was on top of Trish. The security at the shelter broke up the fight and Trish ended up going to the hospital because of her nose. They told her she had to leave the shelter. That's why her and her kids were staying with me. Vee, I'm just letting you know, she falls in love quick and hard. If it wasn't you, it would have been a one- legged dog. Because of her, I will never have another roommate."

I wanted to know why was Anny now telling me this? I asked, "So why you feel the need to now tell me all this?" She said after she kicked Trish out of her home, Trish began spreading rumors about her in the worst way. Even when she was living with Anny, she was spreading rumors and Anny heard of the rumors. She knew it was Trish. After all, only Trish knew what was going on in Anny's household. Anny said Trish denied the allegation, but several people Trish had spoken to had exposed her, and revealed to Anny that Trish was the one spreading the gossip of her life. The main rumor Trish was spreading was about Anny's mom, who Anny loves so dearly. Anny trusted Trish and felt Trish ultimately disrespected her, and for that, she hated Trish with a passion.

Anny said, "Vee, everything I just told you is the truth so help me God. I want to be your friend on Facebook. If you don't, I'll understand." I thought, maybe Anny could be using me to get back at Trish, which I'm sure she was. I asked Anny, "If Trish was such a nasty person, why did you let her stay for as long as she did in your house?" Anny replied, "Vee, she only stayed less than a year, and even before then, I kept asking her if she found a place yet? All she kept saying was that she couldn't go back to her babies' father. She told me he was abusive, and he had thrown her and the kids out. But now, I think that part is a lie." I told Anny that I would add her back on my page. She sent me her number and said to call her or text.

I had a lot to think about now that I got this information. Did I really want to open Pandora's box and call Anny? Did I really need to see what more she had to say about Trish? I didn't call Anny right away. I waited until a few hours later, fighting the thoughts of wanting to know. It wasn't easy. Later, I really couldn't control the urge to know more and so I called Anny. She was cracking jokes right away. I guess it was her way of dealing with her nerves. She then told me of Trish's life story again. Anny also said that Trish was a big liar and that no one really likes Trish like that. She told me to be careful. Man, how many times have I heard that? Damn! Shit just got real awkward between me and Trish.

Even with what Anny had just told me, I just continued to see Trish. I didn't tell her what Anny said nor did I tell her that I had spoken with Anny. After all that we had gone through with people judging us, I just thought it would have been a bad situation. Anny was added back on my Facebook, not right away but a week later. I was hoping that Trish didn't notice I added Anny back. I spoke with Trish that following week. Trish sounded so full of joy. Only if she knew what was being said about her. She was talking about coming to see me but her finances were a bit troubling. I told Trish that I didn't mind getting the hotel. She was relieved, but still had to get a rental. Trish said she would ask her cousin to put the rental under his name because her credit was bad and rental places would not rent to her. Trish claimed her cousin, whom I've never heard of, didn't mind putting his name under the rental.

So all this time when Trish would come see me, she would have a rental, and it would be under her cousin's name? Man, I'm hoping that this cousin of hers isn't some guy she's fucking. At this point, I was starting to think that because her and her so-called cousin would be texting back and forth while she was in hotels with me. I never really bothered to ask her about the cousin because I never expected us to get as far as we did. After I made the reservation for the hotel, I gave Trish the confirmation number. She looked up the hotel on line and saw that it was a four-star hotel and was amazed by the comments the hotel received. She couldn't wait.

CHAPTER EIGHT
"I LIKE YOU, I LOVE YOU"

Finally, the day was here. The day Trish couldn't wait to come. She called early morning and made sure our plans were still on. I was still in the same household with Francis. I lied to Francis and told her I was leaving to Miami today. She was off from work so I didn't worry about who was going to watch Maximus. Trish was texting me every thirty minutes about where she was and how she couldn't wait to see me. I kept thinking about how I couldn't wait to fuck the shit out of her, honest thought. I left my credit card on the table for Francis just in case she would need something for Maximus. I can't lie, it seemed cold the way I was treating Francis. I still loved her, but I was not attracted to her anymore. Like I said, she wasn't strong. She wasn't strong enough to stand up for me. She was a poodle and I was a lion. So different, but I was blessed that she had my son.

I walked out that morning heading to the hotel. Trish was almost there. I wanted to beat her to the hotel. We ended up arriving at the same time. When she pulled up next to me, she came out of the car wearing a long black coat. Her make- up was flawless. As a teaser, she opened the coat to show me what was under it. Nothing but a red thong and matching red bra. She was ready for some passionate sex. We walked into the lobby. I got the key from the front desk, and rushed up to the room to hit that pussy. Trish was a nymph, so was I. Sex was all we had between us, and I was good with that. She didn't waste no time and got right to it.

Once I opened our room door, Trish pushed me on the queen size bed. She pulled my pants off and started licking the head of my penis. She spit right on it and sucked the saliva right back up. Trish was very good at fellatio. This was clearly her specialty. She then engulfed my whole penis into her mouth, touching the back of her throat. It was a sensation of bliss. In other words, her head game was on point. While she was attending to my dick, I was thinking, "I hope she don't think I'm going to eat her pussy." After her performance, I grabbed her thighs and slowly made my entrance into her pussy which was dripping wet all over her legs. The sex was good. I can't say great because it ended too soon. She said "Let me know when you're coming." I felt the sensation, I knew I was coming. I moaned, "Trish, I'm coming!!" She got up off me and grabbed my dick and started sucking it until I came in her mouth. She moaned loudly while swallowing my cum. Oh my, it was something I'd never felt before. I then caught a cramp in my lower right side. It hurt, but the sensation of me coming felt too good. Damn, Trish was good at what she was doing. She sucked it until the last drop. She then put her fingers in her mouth, sucking them one by one as if she didn't want to spill a drop of my cum on the bed.

Wow, I thought. I never had a girl who was this freaky before. She was willing to do anything sexually to please me and that turned me on. I was in love with the sex and Trish was in love with me. I could see it. I know she wanted to say it. After she looked at me in my eyes, she got close to my face with the smell of cum on her breath. She said, "I want to tell you something, but I don't want to scare you away." I turned my head to the side, only because I thought she was going to try to kiss me with cum on her breath. She asked, "Are you going to sleep?" I told her, "No." She wanted to talk, but I couldn't stand the smell of the cum on her breath so I told her, "Let's get ready to go out." She was disappointed because she really wanted to talk. I figured, we can talk at dinner but I didn't tell her that. It was a lack of communication on my part, I guess.

We got dressed and headed out to eat. It was still early. We decided to get something small at a burger restaurant. We didn't say too much to each other at the restaurant. I started the conversation by asking how her kids were. She said that they were fine and spending time with their father. I asked her how her baby daddy was doing and if he approved of her coming to see me? She hesitated," I don't need no approval from that fuck nigga. Man, you just don't know. Only if you knew." I asked, "What do you mean?" She said, "This man has hurt me." She started to tear up. "He kicked me and my kids out of his house. He hit me. He even pulled a gun out on me and shot the gun near my head. He has done so much hurt to me and our kids. I would never go back to that nigga, God can take my life." When Trish said that, she looked so angered. I grabbed a napkin off the table and wiped her tears.

Her makeup started running down from her tears. Our conversation had taken a turn. She then mentioned how her parents were disappointed in her for dating that man and having children with him. She talked a lot about herself and claimed to be the failure out of all of her siblings. She had a younger brother, who was a year younger and was in the military. She also had a younger sister that everyone loved. Her sister was currently in college and making something of herself. Trish then told me about her two other brothers. One was in Rome and the other one in New York. She told me of an older sister who was the worst out of all her siblings. That sister had died when Trish was just a toddler. For some reason, Trish didn't want to tell me how her older sister had died. It seemed too painful for her to even talk about. I thought to myself, how could it be painful? If you were a toddler, then you never really knew her. It started to make me think that Trish was overdramatic. Her tears had gotten so heavy, that people at the restaurant started looking our way as if I was the one that had made her cry. You could hear by the way she talked about her siblings that she loved all of them. All of them, except for her younger sister.

Trish's younger sister's name was Charlina. Trish felt that Charlina was always trying to show her out in front of their father. Trish didn't go to college and because of that, she felt that Charlina would purposely pull out certificates and degrees to outshine her and impress their dad. Trish seemed so disappointed and so sad that her father was not pleased with her decisions in life. I had to ask her, "Do you feel your father loves your sister more than you?" She said, "Yes, he loves that bitch more than me and he cheated on my mom and had Charlina with his side hoe." Clearly, Trish had issues about her father not showing her enough love.

Trish was twenty-eight, seven years older than Charlina who was twenty-one. She talked about Charlina a lot. I started thinking, "How the hell did the conversation go from me asking her about her baby daddy to her sister, Charlina?" I guess these were the people who made a big impact on her life and she needed someone to vent to. I grabbed her left hand and said, "What we go through as young adults, we learn from our mistakes. Let's not dwell on the past and let's think about our future." Her face looked so shocked, surprised. She was blown away with what I had said. I made her feel as if she had a future with me, and she was loving it. She smiled from ear to ear. I told her I'm here to listen and I will listen to every word you say. Oh yea, I know I was getting some brownie points. I didn't want to say anything else to mess up this moment. We got ready to leave. As we were leaving, she said, "Thank you for listening" and gave me a hug. She told me that no one has ever given her a chance to express herself. As she was giving me a hug, I felt an erection. Oh shit, my dick is getting hard. What bad timing. She felt it poking her side. She pulled back and looked in my eyes with a surprised smirk on her face and giggled. She said, "Let's go in the car." We went in her rental and she unzipped my pants and began sucking my dick. Damn, you mean all I had to do was listen? And I get some head?

She definitely made my burger experience awesome. I had it my way. After Trish had her shake to go, if you know what I mean, she said, "Can I tell you something?" I said, "Sure, you can tell me anything." She looked deep into my eyes, grabbed my hands, held tight, and said, "Vee I... I... I love you." It was kinda funny to tell you the truth. I thought to myself, and the Oscar goes to... Trish! I was surprised, wait...actually, no I wasn't. Trish, in love with me? Damn, I like her a lot but I wasn't in love with her. I was tongue-tied and at a loss for words. What should I say? I thought. I did the only thing that came to mind. I said, "I love you too." She wrapped her arms around me and cried soft tears of joy. All I could think of was, what the hell have I done? Why didn't I just be honest with her? After hearing her talk about her babies' father, her sister, and her dad not showing her the

64

love she yearned for, I felt that maybe I could give it to her. Give her that love that she's been looking for. Or maybe, I was just a sucker for a woman in tears.

CHAPTER NINE
"COME VISIT ME"

We went back to the hotel and spent the night together. This became somewhat of a ritual. It went on for months. Trish would visit me in Orlando or Kissimmee, Florida, putting high mileage on her car. She called me every day or texted me that she loved me. Each time she told me she loved me, I would repeat it back to her. I said it so much that I started to believe I loved her. I thought, maybe I can learn to love her. I knew she had a lot of issues, but despite the issues, the sex was gooood!

As months passed by, we would meet up half way on the turnpike at the rest stop and have sex in the parking lot in the back of her car or mine. Her finances were horrible, but she still found ways to come see me. Later on, I found out that she would pawn things like jewelry and many of her valuable items just to come see me. She stopped getting rentals and started driving her own car. Sometimes, she'd even come for a few hours just to hang out. I was ok with that. I spent more time with her than I did with Francis. At this point, Francis already knew I was seeing someone else but she was too scared to ask. She would hint that she knows, but I wouldn't give her an answer. I just always made sure that my son had all he needed.

Sometimes when Trish or I didn't have money to get a hotel. We would spend time in my Dodge Durango (which was big enough to fit fifteen people). We definitely had a lot of sex in my car. We would park near the lake by the Kissimmee courthouse. People would walk by my Durango and see us having sex. I would give the people that were watching a thumbs up, and they would give it back. Trish wasn't shy at all, not by a long shot. She enjoyed an audience. It was like a ritual when we'd meet up at the park, but I could tell she was getting tired of having sex in the car. She would ask when we could go to my place. I always had an excuse. But something told me she knew I was lying.

I finally told her about Maximus. Why I decided to tell her? To tell you the truth, I don't know. She asked me when was he born. I lied and said march of 2010, only because I felt that it would look bad telling her he was born August 18th. Me and Trish had sex on the 19th of August. Oh man, how bad that would look. She asked, "Why you never told me you had a son?" I told her I was waiting for the right time. But really, I never thought that we would make it this far. I wasn't going to tell her that though. She then asked when she would meet him? I thought to myself, "Never!" but I actually told her, "Soon". The questions started coming out about everything now, she was curious. Trish asked, "Do you live with your baby momma?" Oooh shit! What should I say? Fuck it, I lied and told her no. I had to lie. I knew that if I told her the truth, I would lose her. No more fucking and no more head.

She asked all kinds of questions. Like, "When do you get your son? How do you get him? Are you and baby momma cool? How cool?" Oooh my God. I felt like I was in the twilight zone. This day didn't end soon enough. Yes, I lied about a lot of stuff she asked me about. Only because I didn't want to lose her and plus earlier, she had promised to give me some fellatio. I definitely didn't want to miss out on that opportunity. Trish asked me, "Why don't we ever go to your house or apartment? As a matter of fact, you never told me if you had an apartment or house." I told Trish that I had an apartment and I had roommates. Trish never asked me these things before, so I never brought them up. After all this time, she wanted to play detective? We've passed that stage, or so I figured.

It wasn't right for me to lie, but one thing I realized about Trish, she was very sensitive. Whatever information that would hurt her, I tried not telling her. They always say not telling the truth is the worst, but from what I see, telling the truth makes it worse. The thought of whatever you did wrong being brought up in an argument, or her holding it in the back of her mind bothered me. To avoid all that, I just lied. It wasn't the best idea, that I know. Trish wanted to see where I stayed so bad. The next following month, I called Trish and told her I was coming to Miami in a few days. She was happy. She asked, "So where you going to stay?" I told Trish I'd be staying at my mom's house. Trish offered for me to stay with her in her new apartment instead. I said, "Ok, no prob." The wheels were set into motion. I hadn't seen my mom, who stays in Miami, in a while. I figured, I'll see my family, then stay at Trish's place for the night.

The day came when I was leaving for Miami. Once again, Francis was on her last leg. She seemed tired and weak. It was like she had given up. I kissed Maximus and said good bye to them. Francis said nothing to me, but gave me a look of acknowledgement. What was there to hide, I thought. You know, so now what? All she could do was look. Look at me, stare at me, but no words were said. I just left. As long as my son was ok, that's all that mattered to me at this point. I had a long drive to Miami, about a three-hour drive. I knew what I was doing to Francis was wrong, but I felt I needed to be happy. Right now, my happiness meant more to me than being with Francis.

When I arrived in Miami, I contacted Trish. She couldn't wait to see me. I told her I was going to see my mom first, then I would come by her place. She was so excited, but sad because she wanted me to come to her apartment first. I drove to my mom's house, no one was home. I looked around the old neighborhood and saw that a lot of things had changed. I called Trish and asked for her address to the new apartment. She gave me the address. I took my time getting to Trish's apartment because I wanted to do some sight-seeing in Miami. It had been a long while since I drove through my old stomping grounds, and besides, the address Trish gave me was in my old hang out spot in North Miami.

I arrived at her apartment. The outside was very small and it was located in a small Haitian community. I saw her gold Malibu parked outside, so I knew I had gotten to the right place. Once Trish knew I was outside, she ran outside and gave me a huge hug. It felt good getting a hug. Her breast rubbing on my chest felt even better. She kissed me on my lips and cried. She walked me into her apartment. When I walked in, I noticed it was very small. She had a black couch that looked like the couch on a porn video. She had a thirty- two inch flat screen TV and the kitchen was filled with dishes. She was still in the process of moving into the apartment. When I asked her where her kids were, she opened her bedroom door. The kids were sleeping on the floor on top of sheets and blankets. I had never met her kids before, but they seemed pretty cute to me. She had a queen- sized bed that I wanted to try out immediately. The apartment wasn't the best, but it was hers and that's all that mattered.

I went in the bathroom to pee. While I was peeing, I started looking around for any signs of a man staying in the apartment with Trish. She had three tooth brushes. Two kids and one adult. She had two towels hung up on the towel holder. The bathroom was small, literally. After using the bathroom, I went to the kitchen. The kitchen sink was dirty! The sink was split into two. On one side of the sink were pots and plates soaked in bleach, and on the other side were thongs and what looked like white kids socks. This was very nasty, but I pretended like I didn't see it. She kept saying that she just moved in and haven't had a chance to really fix up the place. More like clean up the place, I thought. I asked if there was something for me to drink, she said she had some bottles of water. I opened the fridge and it was filled with kid's food and water jugs. There were bottles of water, some half drunken. I decided I wasn't thirsty anymore.

Trish seemed a little embarrassed, but only because her son had just woken up. He was crying so loudly, "Mommy, I hungry!" She replied to her son, "Go lay down, I'll bring you something to eat." He was three years old, only wearing SpongeBob underwear and no shirt. He had snot coming out of his nose. Her son was making the weirdest noise that I've ever heard. It was like an orangutan, "Aaaaaeeee!". The boy appeared to have something wrong with him, mentally. After she sent him to go lay down, I asked her, "Is everything ok with your son?" Her eyes seemed to glare over, as if I wasn't supposed to notice that he clearly had a disability. She responded, "He's fine, he just eats a lot." She knew that wasn't what I meant.

While me and Trish were talking in the kitchen, we heard the kids crying and fighting. Her son had now woken her daughter up. The noise of her two kids was so loud that Trish ran in the room and yelled, "What's going on in here?" Her son answered, "Lele hit me." Trish yelled at both children. She said, "If ya make me come back in here one more time, I'ma beat both of ya!" I could hear Justin, her son say, "No mommy, no!" Trish slams the door, closing them in the room. I was thinking, these are the horror stories you hear when they talk about dealing with a woman with kids. At this point, I wanted to hightail it out of there!

Trish came back and apologized for her kids. Still I was thinking, damn my plans of getting some pussy tonight had gone down the drain. I didn't even want to spend the night with her anymore. To tell you the truth, I didn't think Trish had control of her kids. They were wild and out of control. After Trish apologized for her kids, her daughter started screaming and crying because the door was closed. She was definitely killing the mood. Her daughter was two years old. That little girl, Gina, started kicking the door while screaming and crying. I must have said, "Oooh hell naw," loud enough for Trish to hear me because she gave me that look like, "Oh no, he's gonna leave me." Trish ran back in the bedroom, this time with a leather belt. All you could hear was a little girls voice saying, "Nooo nooooooo!" then silence... Trish came back upset, but relieved.

I was having second thoughts about spending the night there. Trish grabbed my dick and said, "I really missed you." She put her hands in my pants and started stroking my dick. I asked her, "Your kids are up, how we gonna do this?" She pulled me in the bathroom, looked at her bedroom door, then closed the bathroom door softly. Once the bathroom door was closed, she pulled down my pants and started sucking my dick. This would never get old for me, I thought. I looked at her face. She kept her eyes locked on me while she sucked my dick. My stomach was a little bit in the way. I looked down and realized, damn, I gotta lose weight. Bad time to think about that though. While she was sucking my dick, we heard a door open and tiny footsteps running around the apartment. Trish wanted to go see what was going on out in the living room but honestly, I wanted to finish getting head.

Trish opened the bathroom door and saw her son and daughter running back into the bedroom. They had just taken some cookies from the kitchen. Trish went in the bedroom after them. While in the bathroom, I could hear both kids screaming and crying. The sound of a belt lashing across some child's body. Once again, Gina, Trish's daughter, starts yelling, "Nooooo mommy, nooooo!" and then I heard the sound of an orangutan crying, "Aaaaaaaaeeeee." Damn, this shit was turning me off! What the fuck? I'm in this nasty ass bathroom waiting to get some head and all I hear is some howling cries from kids! Trish came back in the bathroom and apologized some more. She said, "I'm gonna make it up to you." At this point, I want to leave. She started sucking my dick again. I really wasn't in the mood, but I had to fake it so I don't hurt her feelings. After the filacio, I wanted to leave. I really didn't want to deal with this. It was too much of a headache.

I tried to come up with all kinds of excuses to leave. I think Trish knew I was just making excuses. She sat me down, and said, "I don't have a lot. I have two kids that I'm blessed with. I have nothing to offer you but my love and loyalty." Wow, to me, loyalty is everything. When she said that, there was something in me that said, "Give this girl a chance." Then, she did that puppy dog face. How could I turn that down? I stayed that night on her queen-sized bed. It wasn't pleasant because the kids were making noises until about ten thirty that night. I had fallen asleep through their noise, and was awakened by Trish at about one thirty in the morning. Trish was horny and wanted to have sex. How could I turn her down? We had sex until about three that morning. As soon as it was over, I was knocked out, sleeping cold. I woke up at nine AM and everyone was gone. Trish called me. She was at work. She said that she would pass by before I left. I told her that I was going to my mom's house. She said, "If you want to come back at any time, I made you a spare key to the apartment." I was like, what that fuck? When did she have time to make a spare key while we was fucking? The kids were at daycare and there was not much to eat. I told Trish that as soon as she gets out of work to call me.

As I was getting ready to leave, I heard a knock on the door. When I opened the door, it was Trish's sister, Charlina. She didn't look like Trish really. She wasn't pretty either. She had on the shortest "Coochy cutters" that I'd ever seen. Her legs were thick and her body was very well put together. She stood about five six and she had a slim waist. I was already dressed and ready to go. I said hello to Charlina and told her that I'd heard so much about her. She said she heard a lot about me as well. She asked if Trish was home, but I figured that Charlina already knew the answer to that question. I told Charlina that she was at work. Charlina made her way in as if she owned the place. My first thought, this is a setup by Trish to see if I would try to hit on her sister. Clearly, Charlina seemed to have her own agenda. She went straight to the kitchen, grabbed a cup, and poured her some water. I won't lie, Charlina was thick and her ass was amazing. "Oh hell naw! This was definitely a set up." I just kept repeating that to myself.

Charlina seemed nice. She asked, "So, how are you and my sister doing?" I told her that we were fine. She said, "I don't know if you know but my sister can be a bit out of control." I said, "What do you mean?" Charlina said, "Well, I don't really know you but if you tell my sister what I'm about to tell you, you will forever be on my shit list!" Oh man, I coulda easily told her not to tell me and kept it moving, but I was curious. I actually wanted to know. I told her, "You can tell me anything lil sister", in a sarcastic manner. She giggled and said, "Well, my sister has never been a responsible person." She went on to say things like how Trish partied a lot even after she had her son, Justin. She would leave Justin with friends and family just so she could go party at night clubs and meet men. She told me that Trish finally slowed down after she had Gina, but even then, she was still irresponsible. Charlina told me that Trish would leave both kids with her while she went out to clubs and parties at friends' houses.

As I'm listening to Charlina tell me about her sister, I was thinking about how this was my first time actually meeting Charlina. I started thinking, maybe she's telling me these things because she wants to fuck me. Or, she may have some grudge against her sister and wanted to use me to get back at her in some crazy way. However, I decided to use to this info session to my advantage. I asked Charlina, "Does Trish still love her baby daddy?" Charlina said, "No, but that situation was a real disappointment." I asked her, "Why you say that?" She said, "Her baby daddy kicked her out when she had his son. Then she went back to him again and got pregnant a second time, and he kicked her out after she had

Gina. He also put a restraining order out on her." Charlina said, "Trish is the black sheep of the family. She coulda did good by going and staying in college, but she took another route." Charlina said, "I don't feel sorry for her, not at all." I said, "Charlina, but that's your sister, whether she's wrong or right, you gotta always support her." She said, "I know, but how many times is she gonna fuck up? Everything bad that has happened to her, she brought it upon herself."

Charlina seemed adamant. No matter what I said, Trish was a horrible person to her. I asked Charlina, "Do you love your sister?" She said, "Yea I love her, but damn, she just keeps fucking up. I feel like the big sister." Charlina asked, "Did Trish ever tell you about our oldest sister that died?" I said "No, not really, just bits and pieces." Charlina continued, "Well, she died of aids. She was very promiscuous and had a lot of men. Although she was married, she wasn't faithful. She even gave her husband aids. I feel that Trish is heading down that same path." I said Charlina, "What are you saying? Is Trish cheating on me?" She replied, "Noooo, I'm just saying how she used to carry herself. She was heading in that same direction."

Man, with a sister like Charlina who needs enemies. I told Charlina it was nice to meet her but I had to go to my mom's house. Charlina wrapped her arms around my neck and said welcome to the family. Her hug was seductive, very sexual. I put my hand around her back and slowly touched her butt. I know it was wrong, but that ass was soft. She giggled and her hand slowly came down my chest. Oooh shit! This was a sign, a universal sign that this hoe wanted to fuck. Naw, I wasn't gonna do that. She kissed me on the cheek and I pulled away because I started to feel an erection coming on. I told Charlina I had to go and she said, "Fine", and asked for my number. I gave it to her because I was in a hurry, but mostly to get her to leave. Charlina walked out the door looking back. She seemed as if she wanted me to stop her. I closed the door and looked out the window to make sure she had left.

Damn, temptation is a bitch, but I wasn't gonna bite. I wasn't going to tell Trish about what her sister said either, only because I wanted to see if this was Trish's doing or not. Truthfully, I just felt that I should stay out of sisters' arguments. I went to my mom's house. My mom, who is a very strong and strict woman, didn't like me sleeping at no one's house but hers. My mom and dad weren't together. They both had remarried years ago. My mom questioned me about where I went and who's house I was staying at. I gave my mom a smile and hug. In her strong island accent, she said, "This is not a joke, I know you. Miami isn't a place where you can just sleep at anyone's house. These women here have HIV you can't sleep with any woman." I told my mom to relax, I wasn't doing anything. I lied, "Mom, I was at dad's house." She said, "I'm just warning you."

I tried to visit everyone, but Mason was at work. I thought when he gets out, maybe we could go to a strip club. In Miami, it's either the strip club, south beach, or a quick spot to get a drink. Red, he lived too far.

CHAPTER TEN
"TRIGGA, MY NIGGA"

Everyone was either at work or hanging with their wives and kids. Stanley was the only person available. I knew that if I called him, he would keep me out all day.

Stanley was a long-time friend, more like a brother. And every time we got together, trouble would follow. Stanley and I had known each other for over twenty years. He, Red, and Mason were the closest friends from my circle. Stanley was known on the streets as "Trigga." He was that little man standing on my left shoulder telling me, "Do it! Fuck what everybody else thinks." and Mason was the other little man on my right shoulder telling me, "Vee, don't do it! It's wrong. Find another way." It's weird to say it like that, but it's true. One thing I can tell you about Stanley, he has always had my back. He supported my decisions, whether he liked them or not. Stanley was also a lady's man. He got me my first fuck at sixteen, causing me to lose my virginity to some fat girl. The women loved him. They loved his tattoos, dark complexion, and they loved his eyes.

I called Stanley, and surprise, he was home. I told him I was in town. He was excited. He thought I was going to stay the whole week, but I told him it was only for a few days. I went by his apartment that he shared with his girlfriend, Linda. He was finally in a committed relationship. To be honest, I didn't think he would ever settle down. When I started messing with Trish, he asked me, "What about Francis?" I told him the truth, "Things weren't going well, and I'm seeing someone else." Stanley didn't know Trish, nor did he know of her past.

Stanley's girlfriend Linda was a bright skinned, blonde haired island woman, a little on the plus size. While me and Stanley was talking, Linda would listen to our conversation. She didn't like me too much. Only because she felt I was taking too much of Stanley's time, but I hardly see him. Trish called me on my cell while I was talking to Stanley. I told Stanley I was going to have Trish stop by here. I wanted to introduce him to her. The real reason behind it was, if Stanley knew Trish, he would tell me immediately. I was setting myself up. I knew Trish had a past, but I really wanted to see if she and I had a future. I gave Trish the address I was at, across the street from Stanley's apartment. I made sure that I didn't give her the exact address, just in case.

When Trish got there, I went outside to greet her. Stanley did exactly what I knew he was going to do. He took his shirt off and walked right out to where me and Trish was. He gave her a handshake and he said, "If my brother likes you, then I love you. Just keep him happy, you feel me?" Trish smiled and said, "I will." I told Stanley I would come back into the apartment in a few minutes. He said, "Take your time brother. Take all the time you need, but not too much time, we going out tonight," and laughed walking away. As he walked away, Trish asked, "What he mean ya going out tonight? I thought we were going to spend time together?" She gave me that puppy dog face where she looked really sad. I told her that I hadn't seen Stanley in a while. "We're going to hang out for a few hours and then I'll come back to your place", I said. She seemed fine with that.

As soon as Trish left, I went into Stanley's apartment. I waited for his reaction and his opinion on Trish. I asked, "What you think?" He said, "She good for you." I valued his opinion and since he didn't say he slept with her, that was a plus. I know what you're probably thinking. How could I be so accepting of Trish sleeping with damn near my whole high school, yet when it came to Stanley, I was ready to cut her off? Stanley was different. We had a bond. We never let a female get in between us. Bros before hoes.

We got dressed and headed out to a strip club. While we were out that night, Linda was calling Stanley like every fifteen minutes and Trish was calling me about every thirty minutes. Stanley was getting mad that Linda was hounding him so much. Me, I was alright with Trish calling me.

We made it to the strip club. When we got there, it was packed! A lot of people was there. I didn't feel comfortable. As we entered the club, Stanley received a text from Linda. Whatever it was, we didn't stay... Not even ten minutes. We went back in the car and left the club. I asked him, "What's wrong?" he said, "Linda is throwing all my clothes outside." I couldn't help it, I started laughing. He said, "This shit ain't funny!" I said, "Yes, it is!" and continued laughing. Apparently, she was throwing his clothes out because he had decided to hang out with me. I thought, Linda was a controlling ass bitch! But, what could I say? He loved her.

When we arrived at his apartment, I said, "Man, I'll drop you off, but I ain't coming in." He tried to convince me to come in with him, but I didn't. I just told him that I'd see him later and drove off. I called Trish and told her I was on my way. She sounded awake and pleaded for me to hurry.

I finally got to Trish's apartment. It was cold as ice. She musta had the A.C. blowing at 40 degrees below zero. The first thing she said to me when I got there was, "The kids are at their dad's and we are all alone." I went to the bathroom to freshen up. When I came out of the bathroom, she was in black panties and a black bra. She had covered her body with syrup (the one that's used for waffles). I was standing by the bathroom door in shock. Damn, this girl is a nimpho. But I ain't gonna lie, I loved every minute of it.

I took my pants and shirt off. I walked to where she was and started licking the syrup off of her body. I squeezed her breasts together and sucked them like a new born baby. I was sucking her chest and leaving hickies. As I was sucking and licking the syrup off her, I started fingering her. I put three of my fingers in her pussy. She was wetter than Niagara Falls. I laid her down on the living room floor and slid my dick right in her pussy. While I was in the middle of fucking her passionately, I look to my right and saw a big ass roach heading towards my pants. I swear this was the biggest roach I had seen in years. I haven't seen a roach that big since I was fifteen years old. I kept staring at this big ass roach, hoping it would turn a different direction, away from my pants.

I stretched out my leg to move my pants. She thought I was doing some new move because she moaned every time I stretched out. I grabbed my pants with my toes and pulled it away. The roach ended up going to the bedroom. Trish said,

"Let me know if you're coming." I thought she was going to swallow my cum again like she did back in Orlando. I said, "I'm coming!" She said, "Stand up." I stood up quickly and did as I was told. She grabbed my penis and aimed it right on her face. So much cum spewed all over her face. This was amazing, just like a porno. I had never done this before. Her eyes were covered with my cum. And she was sucking whatever cum I had left flowing through my penis. I grabbed my clothes and through them on the couch. I was more worried about the roach coming back. She went to the bathroom to clean up. I went in her room to lay down but thought, where is that roach?

Trish came up behind me. As I laid on her bed, she laid right next to me. She started talking, but I was out like a light. I woke up in the middle of the night having a hard time breathing. Trish was already up. She was concerned, "What's wrong?", she asked. I said, "I felt like someone was trying to suffocate me." Trish gave me an awkward look. I told her, "I need some water". She got up and brought me back a cup of water. As I looked toward the floor, I saw the big roach exiting the bedroom. I was so surprised that she didn't see that big ass roach crawl right pass her. After I drank some water, I finally answered her question. "Nothing", I said. As if it was nothing important to talk about. Trish said, "I hope you don't think it was me trying to suffocate you." I laughed and said, "No, it might have been a roach." She laughed too. "You are too funny." Then we went back to sleep.

The next morning, I had gotten ready to leave Miami a little early. Trish was already on her way to work. I planned to stop by and see Stanley before I left Miami. I called Stanley to see what he was up to. He and Linda had gotten into a fight. I immediately got ready and headed over there. When I arrived at Stanley's apartment, he had his shirt off as usual, so I could see he was all scratched up. I asked, "What happened?" He said, "Linda was upset that I went out last night." She had thrown all his stuff outside. When he got home, they had made-up. A few hours later, some girl texted his phone. Linda wanted to know who it was texting him. He told her the truth and said, "Some bitch that wants the Trigga passion." Linda did not like that answer. She tried reaching for his phone and he yelled, "What the fuck is you doing?" Linda said, "I want to call that bitch and see why she's calling my man!" He said to her, "Man, chill out!" "Shit! Ain't no chilling out, give me your phone!" She yelled. When he said no, she hit him in the face. At that moment, he got enraged and it became a real fight.

Linda went to her aunt's house. Stanley said, "Brother, you know I don't play like that. I don't let no bitch disrespect me." I had to ask him, "Brother, do you love her?" He responded, "Hell yea I love that bitch." I said, "Then the first thing you gonna do is stop calling her a bitch. I don't even like her, but I respect her cause she's your woman. Calm down first and then call her and apologize. As a matter of fact, give me her number." Normally, I would never do this, but for the simple fact that Stanley was my best friend, I wanted to fix this. He gave me Linda's number. I called her and surprisingly she picked up. I said, "Hey Linda, it's me, Vee." She immediately started saying, "Fuck that nigga! He fucking other bitches and treating other people better and with more respect then he do me! I'm fucking done, I'm just done!" I let her vent. I let her say all that she had built up inside her and she let it all out.

After she was done venting, I only had a few words for

her. I asked, "Linda, do you love him?" She said, "Yes, but I....". "Wait", I said. "If you love him, don't throw away what ya worked so hard to build. This hitting, this violence that's going on, needs to stop. Both of you guys need to seek a little help, like counseling. If he agrees, would you go? She said, "Yes." I asked her when she would come home. She said, "I'm scared." I said, "Come home and I will talk to Stanley." She agreed. I spoke with Stanley and he agreed to go to counseling, but only if Linda came home. I let him know that she was on her way back home. He asked me, "Brother, how did you do it? What did you say to her?" I said, "Well, I didn't call her bitch". He laughed. He said, "Thank you brother, I love you man." I told him that it was no problem and just make sure you tell her that you love her as well. As soon as Linda came back, they gave each other a long hug and a kiss. I left after that. I wasn't a doctor Phil, nor a relationship expert. I just gave out my opinion, and I was happy to help them.

CHAPTER ELEVEN
"CRY FOR HELP"

By now, me and Trish had been messing with each other for over eight months. I was still living with Francis, but she was done with me. Still, I couldn't help but to respect her. To her, I've done her wrong. But to me, I just moved on. In reality, I was living a double life. I wanted to be close to my son, that's why I hadn't left yet. I could have easily moved out, but being close to Maximus was more important. I tried doing things to make Francis happy, like taking her to the movies and taking care of all her finances. It didn't work.

I knew what she wanted, marriage. But how could I give her that? I knew we weren't clicking anymore, or maybe I just needed an excuse to not be with her. I wanted my freedom. Being in a relationship with Francis, I felt trapped. We weren't going anywhere. With Trish, I felt free. Like I could do whatever I wanted. We would have long conversations on the phone and in person. We talked about anything and everything.

One day, me and Trish were having a conversation about our exes on the phone. She asked me about Sheila, and even Francis. She said, "Sheila seems like a church girl, why didn't it work out between you two?" I told her because she was too controlling. Then she asked about Francis. I said, "Francis is a good woman, it was me." Trish asked, "What do you mean?" I didn't really want to say anything bad about Francis to Trish, so I said, "It was me. I messed up in the relationship. Things didn't work."

Trish wanted more info and at that time, I wasn't going to give it to her. I turned the tables on her and asked her about her past relationships. She went in saying how she was in a lot of relationships and she didn't want me to judge her. I told her, "Who am I to judge you?" She said she was once in a relationship with a married man who she thought loved her. She even tattooed the married man's name on her back, the upper right side of her shoulder. I said, "Wow, that's deep" but in my head, I was thinking, "Dumbass!" Yes, I was judging, but only in my thoughts. All I could think of was, "The man was married, how you tattooed his name on your skin?" She explained, "I loved him and he was playing me." She told me that it got so bad, her own father found out through friends that knew of their relationship. Once he found out, he was very embarrassed and basically disowned her for sinning with a married man.

I was a little stunned. I asked her how long they were together. She said, "Two years." She continued on about how he was abusive and controlling. She told me that the day he left her, she was devastated. She couldn't eat, sleep, or function. I told her, "Wow, he had a spell on you. Wish I could have that, minus the abuse." She chuckled. I asked her if she ever dated anyone from North Miami? She paused and responded, "Why? What did you hear?" She got so defensive. I said, "You asked me, it's only right I ask you." She said she dated a tall Jamaican guy who was a year younger than us in school. She expressed to me how he was so in love with her. I asked her what happened? She sounded as if she didn't want to answer. She avoided the question. Just kept talking about who he was as a person, but couldn't tell me what went wrong in the relationship.

I've heard the story Trish was telling me before. She had dated a Jamaican guy and cheated on him by having sex with numerous guys from school. The story goes that Trish was supposed to meet up with her boyfriend for lunch. She skipped school with a couple of the football players and they all had sex with her, one by one. One of the football players drove by Trish's boyfriend and sang, "We're gonna fuck your girlfriend, we're gonna fuck your girlfriend." He sang it to her boyfriend as a way of taunting him. To me, this was too funny. I've heard that story over and over, but to hear it come from Trish's mouth, made it so much more real.

She had made a name for herself, and her boyfriend was embarrassed and humiliated. He went from being an "A" student, to failing his classes and smoking weed. Whatever Trish had over that kid, clearly destroyed his world. I stopped Trish, and said, "Look Trish, I know you don't want to tell me what happened between you and your ex, but I already know." She was dumbfounded, but more curious to find out exactly what I knew. I told her what I had heard. The phone went silent, then tears. Trish cried, "Please don't judge me! I know what I did was wrong, I can't change the past. I was young, with no guidance, and low self- esteem." I listened to her and said, "Hey, hey wait. Trish, you're not on trial. That was the past." I asked, "Are you doing that stuff now? Are you fucking twenty, thirty niggas now?" She cried, "Nooo!" "Then let your past be just that, your past. And let's focus on us," I said. She said, "So you know?" I pretended like I didn't know what she meant and answered, "Know what?" "The rumors about me." she replied. I told her, "I've heard the stories, but we are adults now. As long as you're not a porn star or fucking anyone behind my back, then I don't care for that stuff." She was relieved and stopped crying. She wanted to know how long I had known. As if she thought I was using what I already knew to get in her panties.

I lied. I told her I heard it just a couple of days ago by someone on Facebook, which I made up. Knowing her, she was going to search for that person. I lied and kept her looking for a ghost. If I had told her that I heard the story from my friends, then it would have been a problem. A problem I didn't want. I told her she can tell me anything, I wanted to know her thoughts. She was quite upset, saying, "Why are people worried about my business?" I told her, "Don't let it upset you, that's the same way it was for me." We talked for almost four hours that night about our past relationships.

As she was talking about one of her old relationships, I thought I heard her say she was with a woman. I said, "Excuse me?" She said, "Whaaa, what's wrong?" In a shocked, but very excited voice I said, "Ain't shit wrong with it, I wanna know!" Trish described how several years ago, she was in a sexual relationship with a woman that lasted two years. She told me that the woman was a little older than her and a little manly. I asked her, "What did you get out of that?" Her reply was that she could eat pussy good. Damn! Trish was getting too comfortable with me by the way she was talking. I was curious to know more so I asked her, "What happened between you and your gay lover?" She said, her gay lover became possessive and controlling. "We had worked together at a fast food restaurant and it was becoming a problem at work." Damn, now that shocked the shit out of me. Trish came from a church background family, or so she says. How did she fall into loving women?

I asked her, "Are you gay?" she said she wasn't gay, just bi-curious. I asked, "Well, did you eat pussy?" Her tone seemed to change and she said, "Yes." I gave her an example, "That's like a man getting his dick sucked by another man, but still claiming that he's straight." She did not like that comment. She said, "Look, I've done things I'm not proud of, but I'm not gay." She could tell me she wasn't gay all she wanted, but I knew she probably still had gay tendencies. She was still a little upset, but she continued talking. Trish then started telling me about her landlord, a gay woman. The landlord would always try to take advantage of Trish because she was always late with her rent. I asked Trish, "What do you mean that the landlord would try to take advantage of you?" Trish said that when she would be late with her rent, her landlord would want sex as a full payment or at least half a payment for the rent. I asked Trish, "Why don't you report your landlord to the Better Business Bureau?" She started mumbling and never really gave me a straight answer. If I didn't know any better, it seemed as if Trish didn't want to expose her landlord with all the excuses she was giving me. I didn't want to push it any further. I felt she was lying, and it was disgusting me. But either way, I wasn't going to upset her, I just wanted to fuck.

That following week, I went back to Miami for a few hours. I gave Francis the excuse that I had a family emergency. I knew she could tell that I was lying, but I never understood how she continued to accept it. When I got to Miami, I went straight to Trish's apartment. She didn't know I was in town. It was a Saturday morning, when Trish was off from work. I figured, let me not tell her I'm coming to Miami and see what she does on a normal basis. Or, see if there's someone she's fucking on the side. It was like I wanted to catch her fucking or cheating on me. While I was parked outside of Trish's apartment, I could hear a little girl screaming and yelling. It was like she was forcefully screaming her lungs out. I had a copy of Trish's key, but I called her and told her I was outside. She was in disbelief that I was there. When she opened the apartment door, her daughter and son were there and making a lot of noise. Her daughter was crying and screaming so loud, Trish's neighbor was banging on her wall yelling, "Keep that Goddamn baby quiet!" What the fuck? I yelled back, "Who the fuck are you? Motherfucka come outside!" Trish begged, "No! Please, he's just going to call the police. Ignore him like I've been doing all day." I took Trish's advice and ignored the neighbor. As I walked into the apartment, I saw that it was still a mess, oh well.

What Trish's neighbor did really upset me. "He does that because I'm a single mother with no man staying with me", she said. The walls were thin. You could hear the neighbors from both sides talking. The neighbor on the right side, who was banging on the wall, sounded like a redneck, and the neighbors on the left were Haitian Americans. Trish was unhappy that day until I showed up. I was like her knight in shining armor. She was combing her daughter's hair. That's what caused the little girl to go ballistic. Trish told me that when her daughter would cry, her neighbor, the redneck, would call children services or even the police. I asked Trish, "How did she know it was her neighbor that called?" She said she suspects it's him because he would bang on her walls, and then a few hours later, either the police or children services would come knocking on her door. I asked Trish if she wanted me talk to him, but she pleaded for me not to say anything. She told me that she was recording him to show her landlord.

You could tell that Trish was stressing about the situation with her neighbor. It was beginning to take a heavy toll on her, to the point she'd get scared whenever her daughter cried. Her son was more quieter, he just ate all the time, even if he wasn't hungry. That day, he ate so much that he threw up on Trish. She got really mad having to deal with her daughter, her neighbor, and now her son throwing up on her. I stayed just a day, about six hours in Miami. I told Trish, I'd be back. She seemed alone and sad, although she was clearly not alone. I reinsured Trish that I was coming back, it's just all this drama wasn't for me. I drove down to the local burger spot to get a drink and something to eat. While in the restaurant, Trish called and asked if I could come back to her apartment. I went back about an hour later. She had the kids locked up in her bedroom. They were sleeping. Don't know how she managed to get them to sleep this early morning and I didn't ask.

I sat on the couch, which was a little deep in the middle, and kinda uncomfortable. She sat next to me. The look on her face was a very worried look. She said, "Since you've been in my life, a lot of things have changed and I'm hoping that you don't get scared and leave me." I told her that she had nothing to worry about, but that's not what I was thinking. Trish laid her head on my chest and said, "You don't know what you mean to me." I told her, "Why don't you show me?' and I pulled my dick out. Wrong time, I know, but I was horny. She laughed but got right to work sucking my dick. Ten minutes in her throat and I came all in her mouth.

Trish was hot, nasty as she wanted to be. She swallowed my sperm and asked, "Did you eat any celery?" I was trying not laugh. I've never heard anyone ask me something like that. I asked her, "Why you asked that?" She replied, "I was told that when men eat celery, their semen tastes sweet."

She had me thinking now. How much semen has this woman tasted? Eeeew. At that point, I was kinda turned off by her comment. Any man would have been aroused after what she had said, but me, I'm not any man. It was time for me to head back home to central Florida. As I was heading to the door, she grabbed me and tried kissing me on the lips. Hell no! I thought. I turned my head and she kissed me on my cheek. I told her, "I'll be back soon", then grabbed her ass and squeezed it like it was a balloon. On my way back to central Florida, Trish called me. We stayed on the phone for four hours plus some minutes.

She was talking about how she was tired of Miami and wanted to move away from there. I asked her, "What's wrong with Miami?" She said, "She couldn't live in Miami because it wasn't for her anymore." I then asked, "What do you mean not for you anymore?" She started to cry, like I didn't see that coming. She cried that Miami was getting dangerous and where her kids' father lived was a war zone. She told me stories about how there are always shootings there. She feared leaving her kids at his house. She said she couldn't make it in Miami and that she didn't want to end up like her mother, alone and close to death. I've never met Trish's mom, but when Trish said that, I was curious and wanted to know more about her.

Trish pleaded with me, "Please help me get out of Miami. I don't want to die here! I don't want my kids to die here either. Please help us (in tears)." I didn't know what to say to that. I just said, "I'll see what I can do." She begged me, "Pleeeease Vee, I don't want to die here. Help us Vee, we need you, we love you." It was somewhat powerful the way she said it. Straight out of a novel. She had me feeling like I needed to save her. Like I needed to protect her, love her, and her kids. I told her, "Trish, if you're really serious, look for a job in Kissimmee and I'll find you an apartment." She thanked me as if I had already found her an apartment. She cried and said that she loved me. She even had her kids trying to talk to me and they can't hardly talk. All I heard was mumbo jumbo coming out of the kids' mouth. Trish was just so happy, she didn't care. She tried to force the kids to like me and call me stepdaddy. I told her don't do that, but laughed at the same time. She really didn't take me serious because I laughed.

For weeks, she would tell me that she filled out applications at different kinds of places. I guess it was my que to tell her about the apartment searching. Damn, this was getting too serious. Trish really wanted an apartment, and she wanted me to get it. I had to think of something quick. I didn't want her to move from Miami and come stay with me in central Florida. She really wanted to move in with me. What the fuck? I was so mad at myself for even letting her think that it was a possibility. This woman had two kids and a hand full of drama. What was I going to do?

Trish called me while I was at work the next following week. I was a little down because I couldn't think of any way to tell Trish I didn't want her to come. As we spoke on the phone, Trish told me how she was so excited and she couldn't wait to be with me forever. I honestly felt that she just needed a way out and I was her way out. While talking to Trish on the phone, I made up a lie, and it backfired with the truth. I lied and said, "Trish, I was told that you was fucking your cable man and I have proof." She quickly said, "What? No no! Whaaaat, that's not true" I told her, "I also heard from someone that you've been fucking your landlord, getting your pussy licked by her. Tell me the truth Trish! If you tell me the truth, I'll forgive you, easily." That was fucked up what I did, but it was the only thing that I could think of for her not to come up to central Florida with me. I figured, I would have to let Trish go, meaning dump her.

She cried, "Nooooo that's not true! Please don't do this to us!" I told her, "No, you did this to us," and I hung the phone up in her face. That was it, I was free from Trish, or so I thought. She called me more than forty times that day. I felt bad, but it had to be done. Fuck it, this was the only way out. On about the fiftieth call, Trish called me from a different number. I had a feeling it was her, but I wasn't sure, so I answered. When I answered, she cried out, "Vee! Please! Just listen. I'll tell you the truth." The truth, oh shit, this should be interesting, I thought. I said, "I'm listening." Trish took a long breath and said, "There's some things that I've done that I'm not proud of." Again, I said, "I'm listening." She started telling me about a time in her life when she didn't have money to pay her rent and she feared that she would be out on the street with her kids or in a shelter. I said, "Trish, what are you trying to say?" She confessed that she did at one point have sex with the landlord so her and her kids could have a roof over their heads. I was blown the fuck away. This wasn't the end either. She then said that the thing with the cable guy was something that wasn't supposed to happen, it was only sex.

This shit was unexpected, but I had to ask Trish, "Were you fucking the cable man and me at the same time? I need to know so I can get checked." She said, "I stopped having sex with him as soon as we got together." Damn I felt stupid, fooled by the manhoe. I went on further asking her if she'd ever contracted any diseases? Her reply was, "If you really want to know, then, yes, I've gotten syphilis, but I was treated for it." I let out a loud, "What the fuck?!" I asked her, "When were you going to tell me this?" Her only answer was, "I'm sorry." She told me that she didn't have it anymore and said she think she had gotten it from the cable guy. What really upset me is that she says," she thinks." So there was more than one person that she was fucking. All that shit about I love you was an act on her part, and I guess mine as well.

I hung the phone up on Trish. I felt so stupid but I was pissed the fuck off! She called right back and I don't know why, but I answered. She cried, "Please Vee, I told you the truth, I love you! I already gave my boss a one month notice. Please don't do this to me, to us." I rolled my eyes and I hung up again. She just wouldn't stop calling. Had me questioning myself, like, should I change my number? I believe I got what I deserved anyway. I told her I was going to move her up to central Florida, but in reality, I really wasn't. In the end, she did it to herself. I was saddened, and somewhat hurt. I had grown to love Trish, but I was strong enough to walk away.

For weeks, Trish had tried to get in contact with me by email, Facebook, and even contacting my friends like Mason. Mason called me and said, "Vee, what's going on? Manhoe contacting me on Facebook saying she hasn't talked to you in weeks and can I get in contact with you for her." I told Mason only that I decided not to talk to Trish. He advised, "Brother, you playing with fire. For you, I won't respond to her email." I said, "Thank you, bro." he replied, "Don't thank me, just stop messing with the manhoe."

I was back to my regular routine, work and the gym. When I went to work the next day, my supervisor Jimmy informed me that someone had called asking if I was working today. It couldn't have been Trish, because she doesn't know where I work. Jimmy didn't give them any info because they wouldn't identify who they were. I worked as security at a shopping mall in Kissimmee. As I was patrolling the movie theater, a white car with tinted windows pulled up. The white car stopped by my side and the tinted window of the driver side went down. I noticed there were two girls in the car. Oh hell naw! It was Ashley and Trish. I was speechless and shocked at the same time. How did Trish know where I worked? Trish was the passenger. She leaned over Ashley and looked directly in my eyes and asked, "Can we talk?" with tears falling out her eyes and that worried look. My first thought was to curse her out, but something came over me. Ashley yelled, "Give my dawg a chance homie! She drove all the way from Miami at night just to come talk to you in person."

Ashley was Trish's so-called best friend. I had known Ashley ever since we were in middle school, but we never spoke because she had halitosis, bad breath. No matter how many times she brushed her teeth, her breath smelled disgusting. Ashley wore thick glasses and was a tomboy, I almost thought she was gay. I looked at Trish and nodded my head. She came out of the car wearing a "moomoo" dress and flat footed slippers. For some reason, she always walked as if she was stomping her feet. Her arms stayed down at her side and her head was tilted to the side with a worried look on her face. Tears were coming down from her eyes. This was a bit dramatic, even for her. Trish grabbed my hand and begged, "Please give me a chance to explain!" She explained how she never had anyone like me. She told me how in the beginning, she thought I was just trying to fuck. To me, that was bullshit, because she expressed her feelings towards me back then and I've now realized, that was an act. She said, "No! I swear on my children, I love you Vee." She got on her knees and said, "Please just give me a chance." I picked her up and said, "Don't do this here, let's go in the back."

She got up and followed me to the back. Once again, she fell on her knees and begged, crying and holding my right hand. I pulled her up and said, "If you want to be with me, then all the lying has got to stop." She said, "I swear, I swear Vee. I love you." She covered her face with her hands while she cried. Call me a sucker, but I couldn't stand to see her cry. I wrapped my arms around her and said, "I forgive you." In a moment, just like that, I got horny! Bad timing I know, but sometimes I can't control my urges. It just happens at odd times. She felt it poking. I let her go so she wouldn't feel my erection, but she had already felt it. She said, "Damn, now?" We both laughed. What was such a serious moment, had now become a short moment of laughter. She asked, "Are we still going to move in together?" Her giving me the desperation face had me cornered. I said, "Yes, just give me a few days, everything is still on." Trish was getting ready to leave back to Miami. I grabbed her and pulled her into a maintenance room behind the movie theater, where I fucked her. It was a quickie, but a stress reliever. Afterwards she left with the satisfaction of knowing that we were back together.

CHAPTER TWELVE
"MOVING NIGHTMARE, FILLED WITH LIES"

The application for the apartment was approved, but we weren't able to move in yet. Trish had already told her landlord that she was moving out and gave her supervisor at work a month's notice. She had already stopped working when she could've continued working for another two weeks and made some extra money. She had even packed her things and started to empty out her apartment. I called Trish and told her the application for the apartment was approved, and that we should be in the apartment by a week or so. She was upset because she thought she would be in the apartment this week. She claimed she didn't have a place to stay. Just that day, her landlord told her that she'd found someone to rent out her apartment and needed her gone by the end of the week. "That's odd", I told Trish. Her landlord couldn't do that by law. There's procedures the landlord must follow before forcing her to move out.

I personally think Trish was lying so I would have her move into wherever I was living. That wasn't gonna happen.

Trish still didn't know I was living in the same house with Francis. Trish didn't need to know, that's how I felt. Trish decided to put her things in a storage. She was only paying twenty-five dollars a month for the storage, so it wasn't a huge issue. Trish stayed with a relative, or so I thought. Apparently, she was actually staying with her baby daddy's' sister. While I was on the phone with Trish one day, I could hear the kids say, "Auntie." Trish pretended that this lady was her blood relative. I told Trish, "We're starting clean. This woman you're staying with, who is she?" To be honest, I thought it was a lesbian lover. I told Trish, "Please don't lie to me." She said the woman she was staying with was her children's fathers' sister. Damn, I thought. This bitch keeps lying to me. I said, "Trish, why lie about who this lady is that you're staying with?" She claimed that she didn't want me to think that she was still messing with her baby daddy. What she doesn't get is that by her lying, that's exactly what I was thinking. She then started telling me how the kids' father and his sister didn't get along. She must of thought that by telling me this, I was going to accept her staying there. She could hear it in my voice, I wasn't comfortable with where she was staying. But at the same time, lying to me didn't make it better.

Trish was sending pictures and even put me on video chat so I wouldn't have any thoughts that she was doing wrong. She wanted me to see exactly who was around her. Two days later, Trish called me and said someone had broken into her storage and stole a lot of her things. She cried and said, "God, why me?" She called the police, but nothing could be done. It appeared the storage lock Trish had was cut open. Trish cried out, "Why does nothing good ever happen to me? God!" When something bad happened, she always cried out, "Why me God?" When something good happened, it was "Thank you Jesus!" It was crazy, but I really felt bad that her things were stolen from storage. The next day, the apartment complex called and said that the apartment was ready. I called Trish and told her the apartment was ready. She was happy to get out of Miami and start a new life.

I went to the complex to take a look at the new apartment. It was nice. It had one bed room, but it was big enough for Trish and her kids. I signed the paperwork and paid for two months of rent. Trish finally arrived to the new apartment with the kids, but she seemed upset. She and the woman she was staying with had gotten into an argument right before she had left. It was an argument about Trish's children. Apparently, one of them had peed on her bed as well as on the floor in the living room. Also, Trish didn't clean up the mess she'd made around the house. The kids' aunt told Trish that she would never again allow her to come back in her home. Trish was hurt by that, but happy to be out of there too. She unpacked all of her and the kids' clothes in the new apartment. The landlord gave me two keys and I gave one key to Trish. The electricity and water wouldn't be on until the next day though. I didn't stay in the apartment with Trish that night, I told her I was going to work, but really, I headed to Francis' house.

I had gotten a text from Francis saying that Maximus had a high temperature and she needed me to get some meds for him. Trish was not happy that I didn't stay with her that night. The next morning, Trish texted me, wondering where I was and saying that she needed me. I texted her that I was on my way, and that I had passed by Rob's house. Rob was one of my closest friends. He was a tall skinny, sponge bob loving, weird, but hilarious guy. Although he did live in central Florida, I hadn't really passed by his house. When I got to Trish's apartment, I say "Trish's apartment" because I didn't consider it my apartment, she was up and ready to start her new life with me. I had bought her and the kids breakfast, since they'd just moved in. The kids were loud and screaming every hour. I didn't put the kids on the lease and so the landlord didn't know that there were kids living there. I had gotten the electricity and water turned on that day. Trish had a food stamp card that had four hundred dollars on it and she used that to buy groceries for the apartment.

When she filed her taxes, she used her return to buy a flat screen TV. She also bought clothes for herself and bought me a pair of shoes. She didn't buy the kids anything but a McDonalds meal which didn't seem right to me. This spending went on for a month or two until all the money ran out. Trish did show her appreciation by taking me out to dinner at a sushi restaurant. Me and Trish had expensive meals, and the kids had McDonalds, the dollar menu. I would spend a whole day with Trish and her kids, like we were a family. When night fall came, I would go to Francis' house. I would tell Trish I was going to work, but really, I was with Maximus. This went on for almost a year. I would pretend that I was at work, but I'd be at Francis' house.

Francis would wonder why I was out so much as well. I know she wondered why I hadn't left to be with my mistress. There was another woman and she knew. She definitely knew, especially with all her huffing and puffing and no sexing. Back and forth between Trish and Francis was getting me tired. My eyes were red, my body was weak, and it was taking a toll on me. I had to decide sooner or later, but I didn't want to lose my son in the process. Being with Trish from time to time was ok. She would come visit me at work. She even brought me food she'd cooked. Life was good, I thought.

One day, I texted Francis that I would be working late and spent the night with Trish. The sex was better than before. The only thing that bothered me was that her son would wake up in the middle of the night wanting to sleep with us. I didn't like it. He was a little cock blocker, and he pees in bed. Her daughter was weird, an observant little girl. The next night I spent with Trish, while we were having quiet sex, I heard small footsteps and a door slowly crack open. I stopped and said, "I think someone is watching us." The light of the moon shined on her daughter's eyes, and I yelled, "Trish, it's your daughter!" I felt disgusted. Her daughter ran back to her bed and Trish ran after her. When Trish caught up with her, she was in her toddler bed acting like she was sleeping. Trish asked me, "Are you sure she was up?" "Yes, I saw her. I saw her eyes and she looked right at me." I told Trish, "She's not sleeping." Trish seemed as if she didn't believe me but I know what I saw. The next day, I went to Francis' place. I picked up Maximus. Francis was on her way to work, and I had Maximus for the whole day. I decided to take him to meet Trish's kids. Trish's daughter was the first to greet my son, and then her son. Trish picked up Maximus and hugged him and said, "This is my step son, I love you Maximus." I thought that was an odd thing for her to say, especially since it was her first time meeting him. Maximus looked confused, like, bitch please.

I let them play with Maximus for a few hours. As I watched, Trish's son seemed to be a bully. That little nigga tried to trip my son, Maximus, on purpose. I told Trish what her son did, and she spanked him. I liked that she disciplined her son. He seemed to really need it. I wasn't his father, so I'd rather tell Trish and let her deal with him. My cousin Shelly stayed right across from Trish in a two-bedroom apartment. Shelly was what I called a "die-hard" Christian, a bible thumper. Shelly knew of my so-called double life. I guess at the time, I didn't see it as that. I just saw it as me trying to be happy and controlling my life as I saw fit.

One day, Shelly saw me coming out of Trish's apartment and called out to me. Trish peeked out the door, and said, "Who's that hoe calling you?" I said Trish, "That's my cousin, chill out." Trish said, "You sure that ain't one of yo hoes you fucking?!" "Where did that come from?" I asked Trish. She smirked. I said, "I'm gonna introduce you guys in a few." I was starting to see the ghetto side of Trish. Is this what I'm going to have to deal with? Is this the kind of woman I like? Maybe Trish thought I liked that, but I didn't. I approached my cousin, Shelly. I already knew what she was going to say. She said, "Vee, what happened between you and Francis?" I told her, "We aren't together anymore." Shelly said, "Then why are you still at her house?" I asked Shelly, "How you know that?" she said, "Vee, God don't like ugly. What you're doing is going to come back at you hard." I responded, "Cuz, why you always got something crazy to say to me?" She said, "If I didn't love you cuz, I wouldn't say anything." I said, "Ok whatever. Let me introduce you to her."

Shelly agreed to meet Trish. She asked me if Trish was from Miami and I told her yea. Me and shelly walked up to Trish's apartment. Trish came out before I could even open or knock on the door. I said, "Trish, this is my cousin, Shelly, from my mom's side." Trish stuck her hand out and said, "How are you?" Shelly shook Trish's hand and said, "Jesus loves you." What an awkward moment. Shelly told Trish that if she ever needed anything, she stayed around the corner, just let her know. The two had about a five-minute conversation and then Shelly left. She said, "I'll talk to you later cuz." I was glad that Trish got to meet my cousin, but flabbergasted that she thought my cousin was one of my hoes.

Trish was working at a private school with disabled kids in Kissimmee. Before she would go to work, she would take her kids to a daycare that was recommended to her. Trish had a friend forty-five minutes away named Rawshida. Rawshida was Trish's best friend from job corps where they had both attended. I've never met Rawshida in person, only seen her picture on Trish's laptop. Trish told Rawshida everything, meaning everything that happened in her life. There were no secrets that Trish kept from Rawshida. Rawshida was a young, five foot four, long weave wearing woman who was married to a young Hispanic man. I didn't know him well, only that he drunk a lot and was always in trouble with the law.

A few months had passed, and I was still back and forth from Trish's apartment and Francis' house. Trish thought I was working the night shift or working over time, so she never really said much about me coming in and out of the apartment at crazy times. One morning, while I was at Francis', I was just getting up to drop Maximus to day care. Francis had already left for work. After getting him ready and dropping him off to daycare, I headed toward Trish's apartment. It was about seven in the morning when I arrived. I had a key to the apartment and when I went into the apartment, it was a mess. I saw Trish's kids, Justin and Gina, but Trish was nowhere in sight. I thought, maybe she went to her car to get something. Then again, her car was gone. There must be some important excuse for Trish to leave the kids alone in the apartment. Mind you, her kids are toddlers. Gina is only two and Justin is three years old.

I decided to call her cell phone, but it was going straight to voicemail. I couldn't believe Trish was this irresponsible to leave toddlers alone in an apartment by themselves. Justin can easily open the front door by himself, so if he would have woken up and seen that his mom wasn't there, he would've opened the door crying out for his her. I waited for Trish for over an hour, then I decided to call her again. Her cell phone rang twice and she answered finally.

I had so many questions and I needed answers. I was so mad at Trish, but I wanted to hear what she had to say. I needed to know what kind of excuse she had for leaving two little kids in the house by themselves. What makes it worse is that one of her kids clearly has special needs. I pretended to still be at work. I said, "Hey, what you doing?" You could hear it in her voice, she didn't know what to say. She replied, "Um, I'm just getting up. Getting the kids clothes ready for school." Trish was too good at lying. If I wasn't actually at the apartment, she would've gotten away with lying. I said, "Trish, why are you lying?!" Why are you fucking lying to me?"

She was silent for like two minutes, which felt like eternity. I know I lie, but Trish was a pro at lying. I yelled, "Why?" Trish started crying, and I was trying to figure out where she was. She cried, "I'm sorry, I was getting gas for my car." I know Trish was gone for more than one hour, but I yelled out, "You been gone for two hours. What if Justin had woken up?! You know he's got special needs. What was so important that you had to leave your kids by themselves with no adult supervision?! Huh?" She explained to me how she was alone and didn't have gas to put in her car. The kids were asleep and she didn't want to wake them up. She didn't deny the two hours, she didn't even say that I was wrong. Something sounded too fishy. Her excuse was bullshit! It just sounded like straight bullshit.

I had to walk outside of the apartment because I didn't want to wake the kids with my loud talking. As I was talking to Trish, I see her walking around the corner of the apartment complex. She didn't see me, but I could see her. She was speed walking back to the apartment. Where did Trish really go? She didn't drive because I clearly see that she was on foot, but her car was missing. I went back in quickly. I left the door opened for Trish. She cried all the way to the apartment. When she came in, she hung the phone up and saw me face to face. She cried, "I'm sorry! I know you think I'm a bad mother now." Trish wanted me to tell her that she wasn't a bad mom. I told Trish, "It's not me you need to apologize to, and besides, where is your car?" She told me some story about how she was driving to the gas station and ran out of gas around the corner. It was hard for me to believe and I had to find out the truth.

I told Trish to wake the kids up and for us all to go get gas for her car. She seemed worried. Something just didn't sit right with me. Trish was acting funny, like she was trying to buy time. I was rushing them to get in my car, but Trish was taking her sweet time. I cussed, "Fuck!" and took her car keys and walked out. Trish ran out after me, yelling "Wait!" The kids went in my car and Trish sat in the front seat. I drove around the corner where Trish said the car was. It wasn't there. I said, "Trish, where did you say the car was?" She said, "Around the next corner." When I got to the next corner, her car was parked in someone's front yard. The way it was parked, it seemed as if she knew the people who stayed there. I started to get out the car, and Trish yells, "I'll get it!" I yell back, "No, I'll get it!" Her car keys were in my hand anyway.

I gave Trish the keys to my car and walked over to her car. I opened her car and put the keys in and started it up. Yes, the same car she said had run out of gas, had started up just fine. Trish drove off in my car back to the apartment. I looked at Trish's gas line, it was on the second line from the "e". I wanted to know who lived here, and just as I was driving away, a tall, slim, light-skinned man came out the house. I hit my brakes and reversed the car. I stopped right in front of the guy. At first, his facial expression was kinda odd. He seemed as if he was expecting to see someone else, but when he saw me, he seemed disappointed. I said, "Hey, my bad. My wife, (I made sure to yell "wife" so he heard that part) had a problem with her car and I guess she parked it here." He tried to look mean by squinting his eyes and adding some bass to his voice. He said, "Ya, no problem cuz, she can park here anytime." What the fuck? Was this nigga giving me a subliminal message? She can park here anytime? I couldn't even check him because if there's one thing I learned, you never check the guy, you check your girl. It's a universal man code.

I looked at my rear-view mirror and see my car speeding through the block behind me. I gave this nigga one last look and drove back to Trish's apartment. When I pulled up, Trish was just pulling up as well. I got out of the car and said, "Trish, let me know if you fucking someone else right now! You lied and said your car was out of gas, and you got the car parked at some nigga that look like Terrance Howard house! What the fuck is really going on?" I couldn't believe the shit that Trish told me, she's so good at lying. Her excuse was that her car did run out of gas and she was trying to put gas in it before the kids woke up because it's too hard to pump gas when the kids are up. She then said a man stopped and said he would put gas in the car for her. As she waited for him, I called her and she left the car because she knew that I was at the apartment.

Trish's story just sounded like bullshit to me. Early in the fucking morning, really? More like somebody got horny and early nookie happened. I grabbed my keys from Trish, and told her, "You're a damn liar!" She screamed, "I'm not lying, I swear on my life!" I tested her, "Swear on your kids." She said, "I'm not doing that." I got even more upset and yelled, "You can swear on your life but not your kids?" Before Trish could get another word out, I said, "Fucking hoe" under my breath. Out of nowhere, Trish kicked my car and said, "I'm not lying!" and kicked it several more times. I took my car keys out and scratched the word bitch on the side of Trish's car. I threatened, "Continue fucking that nigga, you nasty bitch."

I hopped in my car and started driving off. Trish kicked the back of my car as I drove off, but I didn't care. I was just so angry that I let this bitch play me. As soon as I left, Trish started calling my phone uncontrollably. She left messages saying, "I swear on my kids, I'm not fucking no body! Is that what you want to hear?" In another message, she threatens, "I'm gon give you till twelve noon to call me or come back home, then I'm breaking shit." After about an hour, I returned her calls. I had to wait until I had cooled down because I was just that upset. I saw all the signs. Trish's lies and the things she was saying wasn't making any sense. When she picked up the phone, she was crying. She begged, "Please come quick! Gina hit her head and she's bleeding bad! I don't know what to do."

What I wanted to say was, "Bitch, fuck you and your kids!" but truth is, I was very fond of her kids. Gina was my little princess, and if she's hurt, then I had to be there for her. I told Trish that I was on my way and I was there in less than five minutes. When I got to the apartment, Gina had a slight cut over her eyelid. Her brother Justin had pushed her into the wall. Trish had put toilet tissue over Gina's eye to try and stop the blood flow. I had a first aid kit in the bathroom. I stopped the bleeding, covered the cut with a band aid, and made sure she was fine. I gave Gina a hug and told her to take a nap. She smiled, giggled, and gave me a kiss on my cheek. She's not even my daughter but she warms my heart. As I was leaving, Trish grabs my hand and said, "I swear on my life, my kids' lives, and on everything, I love you Vee! I'm not fucking no one or even looking at anyone." Some people might say I was a sucker for love, but what she said and how she said it, was touching and that's all it took for me to stay the night with her. I had strong feelings for Trish and it was not easy to just rip them out of my chest and lock 'em away. It was something real, or so I thought.

CHAPTER THIRTEEN
"TRISH, TELL ME YOUR STORY"

One Friday night, I had just clocked out of work. I called Trish to see what she was doing. She answered and sounded relaxed. To me, it wasn't normal for Trish to sound relaxed. I said, "What's up? Why you sound so relaxed?" She replied that she was just talking to her mom. I've never seen her mom, only spoken to her on the phone. But from what I hear, she's a bitch. Trish always told me she feared that she would end up like her mom. When I got to Trish's apartment, I asked Trish if she wanted to talk. She seemed a little suspicious and asked, "About what?" I told her to talk to me about anything and everything. Still a little confused, she said, "What, like my life?" I said, "Trish, tell me your story, you know you want to." She said she was scared to tell me because she didn't want me to judge her in a bad way. I assured her that there's nothing she could say that will make me look at her differently. She hesitated at first, but easily gave in. She started off with her mom.

Trish told me her mom was a reflection of her future. She told me how her mom had two kids, a boy and a girl. Just like her mom, Trish had a boy and a girl. Trish said she feared to be like her mom. Her mom grew up too fast and was with a man that promised her the world, but only used her for sex. Trish's mom was a sidechick. Her mom didn't mind being a sidechick, as long as she was getting gifts and being spoiled by Trish's dad. I thought I was listening to another episode of hip-hop wives. Trish said that her dad was a player. He had more women than he could handle. Trish's dad was a well-known drug dealer who was somewhat idealized in the Haitian community. He was also known for trying to assassinate the president in Haiti some years ago.

Trish's mom was impregnated by him twice. He gave her a house, just to take it back from her when she refused to go to nursing school. Trish said her mom left Miami thinking that her dad would come chasing her, but he was too busy chasing and getting other pussy instead. Trish's mom raised her and her brother in central Florida until Trish became too much of a problem child. I thought to myself, "What kind of problem could Trish have given her mom?" I was eager to her hear more of Trish's story. Trish explained that at the age of thirteen, she had lost her virginity to a Hispanic boy who was way older than her. While her mom was out working nights and her brother was out playing basketball, this Hispanic teenager would come over and have sex with Trish all the time. It was even her first time performing oral sex on someone.

At school, Trish was picked on a lot because the other kids thought she was ugly. Trish was a part of the ten percent of blacks that went to a majority Hispanic school in central Florida. She had big ears, a big nose, big lips, braces but with a large gap in between her teeth, and big eyes. She was considered to be the ugliest girl in school and she was often told that. Her mom taught her to wear high heels at a young age. Before the age of sixteen, Trish had very low self-esteem. There was one guy who she thought had liked her. They met at school. He was another Hispanic kid who didn't have her best intention at hand. He was not so popular, but he was well known in Kissimmee. She hardly knew the guy but apparently, he had planned to gang bang Trish. Him and his friends were going to all have sex with her, one at a time. He and a couple of his friends told Trish to come by his house during school, meaning she would have to skip school. Trish did it and skipped school. She was just happy she was getting noticed by guys, whether it was good or bad. She followed him to his house where his friends were waiting patiently. It was twelve guys, mostly Hispanic and mixed guys there. When she saw them, she was scared, but entered the house anyway.

As soon as she entered, the Hispanic kid told her to undress and invited another guy in the room to watch. She was shaking, but did exactly what he said. Trish was nervous and shakened. The Hispanic kid pulled out a condom and put it on. He didn't even pull down his pants, just pulled his penis through the zipper hole. He pushed Trish on the bed and began having sex with her. After about two minutes, the other guy in the room became impatient and yelled, "Hurry up! I wanna fuck too." The Hispanic guy told Trish to get in a doggy style position and began fucking her from the back. He told the other guy to come get his dick sucked. The other guy pulled his pants down in front of Trish and told her to suck his dick. She wanted to be cool with these guys that she'd never met, so she didn't want to disappoint them. She began sucking his dick. He grabbed her head and spit on her face like it was a fetish. After they were done, two more guys came in the room. They began having sex with her too. After they were done, four more guys came in. After every guy finished, more would come in the room. The Hispanic guy kept calling more of his friends. By the end of the school day, Trish had had sex with over twenty something guys she didn't even know.

She felt low, but felt accepted now by the guys. Trish went home and no one knew she had even skipped school, not even her own brother who went to the same school with her. The next day, she was more confident. She thought that she was part of a crew now. Trish thought that her and the

Hispanic kid were a couple now but he wanted nothing to do her. To him, she was hoe and this was something he could not accept. She walked over and talked to him like she'd known him for years. He just brushed her off. She wanted so bad to fit in with everyone and anyone.

When Trish was seventeen, she was walking home from school. A red Honda pulled up near her. The driver was a black man who appeared to be in his thirties. He pulled up next to her and said, "Hey, do you need a ride home?" (In his island accent). Her first thought was to keep walking and ignore this old ass pervert. She knew what he wanted, but went against her better judgment. Trish got into his Honda, keeping her head down. She didn't want to make eye contact because she feared this man who had found some form of interest in her, would think she was ugly. This guy Trish had just met didn't care about her looks. He just cared about how thick she was and how many sexual positions he could get her in.

Instead of the guy taking Trish home, he pretended he had forgotten his wallet at his house and needed to stop there and get it. He told Trish he was going to make a quick stop at his house, and gave her a look as if he wanted to see her reaction. Trish nodded ok. She knew what this guy wanted. She just wanted him to be honest. He pulled up at a wooden house in a low-income area. He told her to come inside the house with him. She got out of the car and entered his home. She walked in. She wasn't scared nor nervous, just ready. He went in the kitchen and brought out a bottle of liquor and two plastic cups. Trish knew he was trying to get her drunk, so she drank the liquor and pretended to be drunk on her second round. Trish wanted to feel loved, and she would get it no matter if it wasn't real. The guy began touching Trish on her thighs and then kissed her on her neck. He then put his finger between her legs. Trish opened her legs wide as if she was welcoming him in her vagina. She really thought this man that she knew nothing about or ever seen before, could love her. Trish explained she had low self-esteem and was trying to get love anyway she could. Then she stopped and went on to another story.

I didn't want to hear anymore of her story because me and Trish were together. I know I asked her for her story, but I guess it was a little too real for me. How can I be intimate with her knowing these things? How can I kiss her when I know that her lips have been on plenty of other penises? Who wants to hear about their girlfriend being a hoe? Trish seemed eager now to tell me more of her story. I didn't want to offend her by not being interested in her story, but I was getting disgusted. I looked at Trish and pretended to be interested.

She told me she had run away from her mom's house in Kissimmee to be with a man who she claimed she was engaged to. Another man she had met on the street of central Florida. She claimed he picked her up at a corner store, where he offered her to have a drink with him. He was a little older she said, about three years older than her. He had his own car but still lived with his parents. Trish said he took care of her, bought her food, and always asked if she needed anything. That's what she liked about him. He always showed he was concerned about her. Trish said after she introduced him to her mother, he proposed to her and she said yes. Trish's mother wasn't too pleased with her decision, but Trish felt she was an adult. As Trish was telling me the story, she never said his name. She had me thinking, it must be someone I know. Oh God, I hate the feeling of walking by someone I know and he'd had sex with my girl. It's an awful feeling.

Trish told me he gave her a gold-plated diamond ring. She thought the ring was real and she showed it off to friends and family. One of Trish's friends said, "Wait, let me see." The friend said, "Girl, this ain't real! This is cubic zirconia and it's not gold either." Trish said she was embarrassed that her so-called friend put her out there in front of people. She argued with her now ex-friend, and went to her mother's house crying to her. She told her mom that someone said her engagement ring wasn't real. Her mom grabbed her ring finger and pulled the ring off. As she pulled the ring off, there was a green stain around her ring finger. Her mom yelled, "Oh Lord, give me the phone! I'm going to call him right now." Trish gave her mom his number and she called cursing up a storm when he answered. Trish said her mom told him, "My daughter is not a bum bitch and she deserves better!" The next week, he got her a real ring, but it was small and cheap. At least this one was real.

I asked Trish, "How did the relationship end between you and him?" She said the last straw was when she went over to his house. His mom had let her in while he was at work. Trish said his room was a mess and she decided to clean it for him. My first thought when Trish said she decided to clean his room was, "Bitch, you can't even clean up your own apartment!" But that's none of my business. She said when she started to pick his clothes up off the floor, a few papers fell out of his pants. They were full of phone numbers of other women. She even found condoms and a hotel key. Trish was hurt. She was even more hurt when she called the numbers of the girls and found out he had been in relationships with all of these girls while engaged to Trish. She claimed that after that, the relationship was over. But something didn't make sense, so I asked Trish, "Did you ever confront him about those numbers?" She said she did, but didn't want to get into details. I thought, this was some bullshit ass story to make herself look like a victim, but I wasn't going to tell her that. I asked Trish, "So a lot of your past is in central Florida?" She answered, "Yes and no." She said, "The difference between central Florida and Miami is that the guys here in central Florida don't talk about who they fucked. The guys in Miami spread the word. "She was somewhat right about that, I guess.

She told me she went to Job Corps in Miami. When she would leave the campus, she would see the security guard who worked the front gate. Trish immediately fell in love with him, or so she claimed. While she was talking to me, I started seeing a pattern of a girl who was too eager to fall in love and be loved, but going about it the wrong way. I wondered, was her cycle repeating itself again with me? She began seeing this security guard, who's name she didn't mind telling me. Mark was his name. Trish was so much in love with him, but it seems Mark was in "like" with her. He didn't love Trish, he liked her. At first, Trish said it was after two days that Mark fucked, but later, she changed it to a week. I guess she didn't wanna look like a hoe. My facial expression said it all! Why lie about it? It's already on the table. But once again, I didn't say nothing to Trish, I just listened. Trish said, after a few months of having sex with Mark, she still had never been to his house. They would only meet up at hotels on the weekend. Trish said she knew something wasn't right, but never asked Mark.

One day, Trish found out from some people at Job Corps that Mark was a married man. The rumor had traveled so far, even her father had heard about it. Trish's father was so upset that he basically disowned her when he found out. Trish confronted Mark, and he confessed, "Yes I am." He got caught and was quickly going to end his sexual relationship with her. Trish cried. She didn't want their relationship to end. Mark told her, "I was not happy because me and my wife were going through some problems, but now we are working it out." Trish asked Mark what could she do to make things work between them? She would do anything to continue the relationship. Mark said, "There's nothing you can do, I'm married." She was devastated.

While Trish was telling me this, I thought, "Wow, she really has issues." Trish had a tattoo on her back that she had previously told me used to be her ex boyfriend's name. I asked Trish, "Is that his name you tried to cover up with a butterfly on your back?" She looked shocked, like I wasn't supposed to ask that question. She asked me, "You can see it?" I said, "If you look hard enough, you can see a name, and it starts with an 'M'." This girl didn't even remember that she told me about the tattoo when we first started dating. She said, "Yes," and hung her head in shame. I asked, "When did you get the tattoo? After you found out he was married or before?" She said it was before she found out, but I believe otherwise. Trish was a liar, some of what she told me might be true but the rest just didn't make sense. I told Trish that was an interesting story, but in truth, I was disgusted and started wondering things to myself. Should I treat her like a hoe or a girlfriend?

Trish started talking more about her life. Damn, I thought she was done. Now she starts to tell me about when she was in a lesbian relationship. I don't think Trish remembers that she had previously told me about her lesbian relationship but I quickly sat down for this. I wanted to hear if the story would be the same as the other story she told me. Trish lied so much that she didn't remember the things that she said. Trying to keep up with her lies, she ended up forgetting a lot of the stories she had already told me. She saw my face when she mentioned lesbian and she giggled as if she thought being in a lesbian relationship was cute. As if it was all men's fantasy.

While she was in Miami at age twenty-one, she had gotten into drugs. Drugs like cocaine, weed, and pills. She was working at a burger joint. There, she had met an older woman named Bertrice. Bertrice was a 5"9', heavy set, black woman who befriended Trish. Bertrice played a mother role to Trish. At this time, Trish was living from place to place. She had left her mom's house and her father had disowned her. She didn't have a permanent place to stay. Trish told Bertrice she was living with friends that she didn't get along with. Bertrice told Trish she could live with her until she found a place of her own. Trish said while she was living with Bertrice, Bertrice finally made a move on her. Trish wasn't paying for rent, lights, or water. Bertrice felt she had to get some form of payment. Trish said Bertrice came in her room and said, "What are you watching?" Trish answered, "Pretty Woman." Bertrice said, "That's my favorite movie." Bertrice laid right behind Trish, and pretended to watch the movie.

Trish said she always knew Bertrice was gay, because everyone at work talked about it. Trish said she was a little scared and nervous. Bertrice laid her arms on Trish's thighs and started caressing them. Trish said she didn't know what to do. Bertrice turned Trish on her back, pulled off her pajamas, and sniffed her pussy. Trish said she closed her eyes and imagined it was a man. Bertrice started kissing her thighs, then slowly kissed her pussy lips softly. Trish said to me, "I ain't gonna lie, that shit felt good." I looked at Trish and thought, once gay, always gay. Was this the same woman who was reading her bible just a week ago? Damn, Trish was a good actor. I truly believe she's still gay though. After she made that comment, that sealed the deal. Reading the bible like she was all holy? Talking about she wants a man she can go to church with? Oh hell naw. She was confused in the worst way.

Trish said after that night with Bertrice, they were in a relationship. Trish remained with Bertrice until she started stripping. That's where she met Cinnamon. Cinnamon taught Trish the ropes of stripping. Bertrice hated Trish working so late. And when she found out Trish was spending a lot of time with Cinnamon, Bertrice was so mad that she threw Trish's things out of her house. Trish called Cinnamon and moved in with her for the time being. Trish and Cinnamon got real close, sexually. Trish wasn't a pretty stripper, but she had an ass the clients liked. Trish saved up one thousand five hundred dollars, and hid it under a carpet in her room where Cinnamon let her stay. Trish said, one day she had taken one of Cinnamon's clients and Cinnamon wasn't too happy about that. Cinnamon and Trish got into a fight at Cinnamon's house. Cinnamon's friends were there and they all jumped Trish. Cinnamon told Trish to get her shit and get out her house. Trish received a bad beating that night and walked away limping to her room to collect her items. I honestly think there was more to the story that she wasn't telling me, but I let her continue. Trish had money saved, so she didn't worry. When she looked under the carpet, her money was gone. Cinnamon kicked Trish's room door open and said, "Don't worry about that money, that was everything you owed me, hoe!"

Trish was broke once again. She tried to go back to Bertrice, but Bertrice had moved away. Trish walked the streets of Miami for a few days until she met an old man in a wheelchair who offered her a place to stay. Trish didn't know the man, but she needed a place to stay and a place to bathe. The man in the wheelchair allowed her to stay, as long as she took care of him physically and sexually. She agreed. He was paralyzed from the waist down but still wanted sex. She didn't know his name nor his age, just knew he was old and couldn't walk. I was intrigued by her story now, it was getting interesting. She said when she performed oral sex, he couldn't feel it. When she got on top of him and began to straddle his dick, sometimes he peed and didn't realize he peed inside her. She felt disgusted, nasty.

I had to ask Trish, "Why didn't you go to your family? Why didn't you go back to your mom or your dad?" She said one word, "Pride." I asked Trish, "At what point do you say fuck pride? You needed some help." She replied, "My family don't care about me. My mom maybe, but my dad, hell no!" I was shocked, "Trish, that's an awful story. What happened to the old man in the wheel chair?" She said the last time she saw him, he had called the cops on her and had her thrown out of his house. I was shocked. I said, "What!" She told me how she went to jail for kicking the old man's wheelchair. I broke down laughing and asked, "Why did you kick his wheelchair?" I was curious. She replied, "He tried to trip me when the police wasn't looking." I fell down laughing. Trish said, "That shit ain't funny." I paused, slowly stopped laughing, and thought, "Wait, ain't he paralyzed?" I said, "How he tried to trip you if he couldn't move his legs?" she said, "He managed to move them that night."

Trish had issues. Even Jesus himself would have ran the

other way. I thought about all these men Trish has had an issue with. They have damaged her. Now it makes sense, or so I thought. I'm not a doctor, but it seemed as if Trish was looking for a father figure. Someone to replace her father and the love she yearned from him. I stopped laughing and got serious with Trish. I asked her, "Trish, where were your brothers? Do they know what you have gone through? Why didn't they help you?" Trish gave me a blank stare. She said that her brothers only cared about themselves and what they had going on in their lives at the time. As she said that, I remembered what Trish's sister Charlina said to me a while back when she came by Trish's apartment that day. Trish was an irresponsible person who only cared about hanging with friends and partying. Trish would leave her newborn with Charlina while she went out clubbing.

What Charlina told me, had me believing that Trish's family saw her as an irresponsible person, pretty much a fuck up. They didn't want to take any risk on her. Trish continued. She talked bad about her oldest brother. She claimed that at the age of ten, when she was living with her dad one summer, her oldest brother raped her. Her voice started getting shaky like this was something hard for her to talk about. I thought, damn, Trish just finished talking about all the guys that had taken advantage of her and all the crazy shit she had gone through. How she had been used and abused. And she wants to start crying...now? I know that's a touchy subject to talk about, getting molested and raped, especially by a family member so I listened respectfully. She told me about one night when she was asleep and her big brother came in the room. As she was telling me her story, she started crying. She said he held her mouth shut with his hands placed over her lips. He opened her legs with his free hand and forced his way inside her. I asked Trish, "What did you do after he was done?" She said she told her dad the next morning. Her dad didn't believe her. As a matter of fact, he threatened that if she ever repeated it again, he would disown her.

Later, Trish told her mom when she went back to her mom's house. She said her mom called her dad, cursing him and the older brother out. I said to Trish, "That's good and all, but did anyone call police? She shook her head, "No." I was flabbergasted. I wanted to know, "Trish, why didn't they?" All she said was that it was hard to explain. Her oldest brother did not share the same mother with Trish, so it wasn't clear to me why her mom didn't call police. She still couldn't give me a straight answer, so I just thought to myself she had to be lying about something.

Trish felt so comfortable, she even got into the subject about her having sex with thirty guys, just like what Red said. The story he told me was accurate, because she said exactly what Red had said, except that she didn't remember the guys she fucked. She claimed she remembered some of them and that she was on drugs at the time, which was a lie. I know she added the drug part to make it look like she was under the influence. Bitch please! I said, "Trish after having sex with those guys, how do you manage to befriend their girlfriends?" She looked at me strangely like, "How dare you ask me such a question?" I continued, "I mean, you're close with all the guy's girlfriends. Are you just waiting for the right time to tell them, I fucked your man? I mean, what is it? Tell me."

She burst out crying and dropped her head in her arms, covering her face. She cried, "Oh my God, oh my God." She said, "Vee, if I could take it back I would. How can I live with myself?" I answered her, "one day at a time," and placed my hand on her back. I apologized, "Trish, I'm sorry for saying it like that." she accepted, "no, don't be sorry." She wiped her tears and said, "I pray to God that you don't judge me of my past Vee." She begged, "Please don't judge me." I told her and I told myself that I wouldn't judge her, but honestly, it did sit in the back of my mind. So, this was the story of her life. She's been through it all. Alcohol, drugs, men, and women. "What haven't you done?", I asked Trish? She replied, "Marriage." One word, marriage. She's done it all but marriage? When she said that, she looked at me as if I was supposed to respond. With what I knew about Trish, how could I marry her now? Who would marry her? Would she go back to her old ways? Is it true what they say, "Once a hoe, always a hoe?" I just couldn't see it happening because of who Trish was, or used to be. Taking a chance on her would be a huge gamble. I've already went as far as fucking her and bringing her to central Florida, but marriage was not in my vocabulary.

CHAPTER FOURTEEN
"STICKS AND STONES"

Me and Trish were arguing every week about the house not being cleaned or about how sex was less and less now. We went from having sex every day, to once a week, and then three or four times in a month. She chose not to give me sex as way of her punishing me. That was stupid, I thought. Trish had a weird way of doing things, and to me, this was one of them. If she was going to act like that, I was gonna get it somewhere else. Not that I had women lined up, but she wasn't the only pussy in town.

The nights I spent with Trish, she would get up in the morning mad at the world. It got to where she was mad every day. Things weren't the same. We were calling each other names. Bad names, like "bitch", "fuck nigga", "hoe", and "bitch ass nigga!" I even called off her imaginary wedding that she really thought was gonna happen. Yea, I know that was wrong for me to string her along. I felt the imaginary wedding was the only way to keep her in control. She screamed, "I don't give a fuck!" Little did she know that this was already planned all in my head, premeditated. She was unstable. I couldn't see myself marrying Trish and I really didn't want to. Being with her forever? Hell no! But I could see myself fucking her forever.

It was like, neither one of us wanted to back down during our arguments. It was either she had to scream to express how she felt or I had to yell to get a point across. Most of the time, we didn't speak for a day or two. When Trish would give me the silent treatment, I stayed at Francis's house. Francis would always figure something was wrong when I would be home on days I'm usually never home. She'd ask, "Is everything ok?" and I'd always tell her, "I'm good." I wouldn't go back to Trish's apartment until she called or texted me. One day, Trish texted me to come by after work. When I'd be gone for two days, Trish figured I was at Rob's house, or so she thought. I figured Trish knew I was at Francis's house when I disappeared. Even though she never spoke it out loud, I knew she had a feeling. When Trish texted me to come over after work, I'd wait for two hours then appear at her apartment.

One day, when I got to her apartment, she was upset. It was about something her sister Charlina had told her. I noticed Trish had on tennis shoes and sweats on when I came to see her. I had a thought that she was ready to fight someone because she sure didn't work out. She stood in the shadows with her eyes glaring at me. Trish said to me, "Take a seat." I asked, "What's wrong boo?" Trish replied, "Naw, ain't no boo here. Sit yo ass down right here!" I was confused. My first thought was that she knows that I'm staying with Francis and wants to finally put it out there. My heart was pounding. Trish said," I spoke with my sister and she told me you tried to fuck her a while back in Miami in my old apartment. I didn't believe her, but that bitch screen shot your number to me! See, I never gave anyone your number. So tell me she's lying. And if you lie, I swear to God I will fuck you up right here!"

Usually I'd be turned on by her aggressiveness, but what she told me her sister said had gotten me upset. I told Trish the truth, "You had gone to work and your sister came over. She told me how you fucked your own life up, how you made dumb decisions, and how you continued making dumb decisions." I told Trish, "I didn't try anything with your sister." Trish then said her sister told her that I grabbed her butt. I said, "Trish, if I did that, why she waited all this time to tell you?" I did grab her ass, but I wasn't going to tell Trish that. Trish got up off her seat and reached for a leather belt. I started laughing, only because I couldn't believe what I was seeing. Like, is this bitch really gonna try to whoop me? Like a child?

Trish said, "You think this shit funny huh?" I told Trish, "Look, you don't have to believe me, but tell me if I'm wrong. Charlina said you went out to parties a lot and she watched your kids while you were at the parties and clubs. I know I should have told you as soon as she said those things, but I didn't want to ruin you and your sister's bond. And besides, she's your sister. Who would you have believed at that time?"

Trish paused, dropping the belt and picked up the phone to call her sister. She cursed Charlina out on the phone and even threatened her. I could hear Charlina saying, "He's lying!" but Trish was responding back asking, "How did he know all the info he knows then? Trish tells her, "Only you and I knew these things," and hung the phone up on Charlina.

Trish called her brothers and told them what Charlina

had done. She then called her mother and told her too. Trish and Charlina didn't have the same mom, just the same father. Trish put her mom on speaker and I heard Trish's mom say, "Fuck that bitch and her mom too." I was still sitting there waiting for Trish to get off the phone. When she saw me get up off the chair, she told her mom she would call her back. Trish then said to me, "You and my sister should have never been that close. You don't even know that bitch like that." I agreed, "You're right Trish, I'm sorry." but Trish just kept on going with it for almost two hours straight.

While she was talking, I fell asleep. I was so tired I immediately pass out. When I woke up, a whole day had passed. It was already time to go to work. Trish was in the kids' room, still upset about me and her sister. I said, "Bye" to the kids and Trish. Trish ignored me, but the kids said, "Bye Vee." I thought to myself, what made Trish's sister tell her those things? I was curious, but I wasn't going to ask Trish.

After work, I went by Trish's apartment. As I was walking towards the apartment, I could hear Trish talking to one of her friends on the phone. I didn't realize how thin these walls were. I could hear Trish's conversation. Trish was so loud, her voice carried through the apartment complex. Trish said, "Yes Darlene, do you know she told my boyfriend everything? She was talking about how I'm a bad mother. And him, I don't respect his ass at all girl! He ain't no man."

I was hurt. I understand Trish was still pissed off about that situation with me and her sister, but now she was degrading me in front of her friends, probably to her family as well. I was so mad, I quickly opened the door and said, "Is that how you feel?" She hung the phone up on her friend and asked, "What are you talking about?" I was pissed. "Don't try me like I'm stupid! You? Don't respect, me? That's fine. I'm out of here! You can talk shit about me when I'm gone." Trish burst into tears yelling, "I'm sorry!" and grabbed my hand. I said, "Trish, why you have to degrade me to your friends? I've never done that to you." She pleaded with me while in tears, "I'm sorry." At this moment, I'm feeling gassy. I needed to take a shit. I pull my hands away and told Trish, "When I'm done using the bathroom, I'm out."

I rushed to the bathroom, pulled my pants down, and dropped a load of shit. Trish opens the locked bathroom door with a butter knife while I was shitting. I yelled, "What are you doing?" she cries out, "Please Vee, I'm sorry! What do you want me to do? I'll do anything, please!"

Right then and there, I wiped my shit filled ass with a tissue. I presented her the tissue and asked, "You'll do anything huh?" She looks at me and says, "Please Vee, anything but that." Now, I know it sounds nasty, but I've always believed that if you gonna talk shit, you might as well eat shit. I said, "Eat this shit." She hesitated a bit, then stuck her tongue out and closed her eyes. She was so close to tasting my shit. I thought to myself, "I can't believe that this girl is going to eat my shit for real!" And the craziest thing about it, something in me wanted to see her eat it. But I stopped her. After all the bullshit, lies, shit talking, her temper, all the shit I had to endure, I wanted her to eat that shit. But I just couldn't do it. I couldn't allow her to put my shit in her mouth.

I said, "Stick your tongue back in your month." She opened her eyes and looked at me. I couldn't let her eat the shit. For her to come that close to doing it, she must really love me. Maybe I still loved her, I thought. She wrapped her arms around my waist and apologized, "I'm sorry, don't leave me!" I thought to myself, you were about to eat my shit, and yet you're begging me to stay? It was weird, but once again, I stayed. After that, I cleaned myself up and washed my hands. As I watched Trish brush her teeth, I thought, damn, I was wrong for almost allowing her to eat my shit. At the time of anger, you hardly think straight. I knew things would never be the same. We never spoke about that day again. How did Trish feel about me now? I didn't know.

I knew she wanted marriage, but more than that, she wanted to let the world know that we were together. I wasn't ashamed of Trish, but she felt like I was hiding her from people we went to school with. As if showing them we were together, was a way of somehow cleansing her past. Trish would not let go of her past. To me, this was her downfall. Trish especially wanted people from our high school to know that she and I were a couple. I realized it wasn't really the whole world, it was specifically the people from north Miami. It was awkward to me how that was all she wanted, and when I confronted her about it, she became upset and cursed, "Fuck north Miami! You're ashamed of me and my past." I said, "I took you out. I held your hand in public and what did you say to me? You said that I wouldn't have done that in north Miami. So I can only guess from your statement, you just want north Miami people to know we're together." She walked off pissed, saying, "You don't understand."

I decided to leave for that day. I told Trish I was heading to work, but I was really going to Francis' house. Francis was upset. Damn, I felt like everyone was upset with me. Francis didn't like that I wasn't around as much anymore. She even said, "Don't let your bitch stop you from seeing your son." I gave Francis no response, only because she was right.

About a week ago, as I was sleeping at Trish's apartment, I had a strange feeling that caused me to wake up. It was about six o'clock in the morning and a thought came to my mind. I decided to go outside and check on my car. As I quietly opened the door, not waking Trish or the kids up, I saw a figure near my car. When I got a little closer, I realized it was Francis. Oh shit! What the fuck is she doing here? My heart pounded, my feet almost gave way, I slowly stopped breathing. My first thought was to hide, so I hid behind the bushes. I observed Francis open the car door and start to take things out. I couldn't see clearly what they were, but I was just hoping she didn't come and knock on the apartment door. She then walked up to Trish's car and started taking items out. All I kept thinking was how did she know where Trish lived and even more surprising, how did she know which car Trish drove? I waited until she was done and watched her get back into her car and drive off. A couple days later, Trish frantically came in the apartment. She was upset and claiming that someone had broken into her car and stole all her makeup bags. I wondered, is that what Francis took? But I wasn't gonna say anything. Just trying to keep the peace.

I was caught and thought that this was the end for me. I didn't wanna go back to Francis' house, but I couldn't leave my son. I decided that I was just gonna man up, and go over there like nothing had happened. Every day I waited for her to confront me, but she never said anything. I didn't get it. Why would Francis allow me to continue this double life? I figured, if Francis don't say anything, then I won't say anything.

Trish called me leaving messages saying things like, "You see me calling" or "If you don't pick up, I'll be at your job." Trish called over twenty times that night. I had to put the phone on vibrate. It was almost time for me to go to work, so I grabbed my uniform and headed out. Trish continued calling, leaving voicemails and texts. She was saying things like how she was going to keep calling until I picked up. I liked the aggressiveness and the attention I was getting from Trish, but it was getting to be too much.

As I was working security at the shopping mall, I received a text from Trish that said, "I'm here at your job." My heart started pounding, not because I feared her, but because I was afraid she might cause a scene and cost me my job. I finally responded and Trish texted back, "Oh, now you texting back huh?!" I told her I was busy tending to a situation, which was a lie, but I had to think of something before she started acting up at my job. She texted me that she was by my car. Oh lord. I was working alone, so I had the opportunity to go see what was up with Trish. When I got around to where my car was parked, Trish was on top of my car. I was mad as fuck. I yelled, "You crazy bitch, get the fuck off my car!" She replied, "Fuck you nigga, I'll break yo shit! Try me if you want." As I got closer to Trish and my car, I noticed Trish had a crowbar in her left hand. I said, "Trish, why you acting crazy for?" She replied, "You think you gonna leave me? You got me fucked up!"

She started jumping up and down on the hood of my car. When I got closer, she raised the crowbar up as if she was going to hit me. I backed up, just in case. I could've called the police and had Trish arrested, but I cared about her too much to do that. She had kids, and I've learned ever since I was a child, if you called the police on a loved one, there is no coming back from that. You don't ever involve the law in your dispute. That's why I didn't call the cops when I had the chance. I said, "Come down from my car now!" She said, "Fuck you nigga, come make me!"

I ran where Trish's car was and said, "If you don't, I'ma flip your car over." She started yelling, "I fucking dare you bitch!" That's all I needed to hear. I bent my knees and grabbed underneath Trish's car. Slowly, I started getting it off the floor. Trish jumped off my car and said, "Wait! The kids are in the car." When I heard Trish say that, I dropped the car down. I saw Justin and Gina, Trish's kids, in the back seat. They were lifting their heads up and crying out to their mommy. Trish yelled, "You see what you've done?" and opened the back door. Gina, Trish's daughter ran towards me, and Justin ran to Trish. The kids cried, and so I offered to take them to get something to eat.

I would ask Trish, "Why are you so mad all the time?" She said, "Vee, the things you say to people are enough to cause them pain. Not physical, but real mental pain." I said, "Trish, I hear what you are saying but I would like to come home to a clean house and a cooked meal. I ain't asking for much, Trish. You think by me saying that the house is nasty, that I'm being verbally abusive?" She said "No, that's not true. You've called me a bitch, hoe, and the worst, you've called me a bad mother." She said, "Vee, do you know what that does to a woman? For someone that's supposed to love you, tell you you're a bad mother? It hurts Vee." At first, I didn't remember saying that she was a bad mother, but then it hit me. I didn't call her a bad mother, per se. What I said during a heated argument was, "I'm glad we don't have kids together. Don't need you slapping me with child support." It was her actions that had me questioning her ability to bare my children.

When Trish would buy expensive sushi for herself, she'd buy a dollar menu meal at a fast food place for her kids. She'd spend over five hundred dollars on clothes for herself, but when it came to her kids, it would be less than a hundred dollars. It was also the way she conducted herself when the father of her children would deposit what little money he had in her bank account for the kids. As if she depended on it and needed to live off of the child support money. It was just the things I saw Trish do that I felt were bad parenting, in my opinion.

Something else I noticed was that Trish favored her son, Justin, more than Gina. Justin had a disability that was clearly visible. One day, when Trish was calm, I asked her, "Does Justin have a disability?" She said she didn't know and she was too scared to find out. Apparently, people have always asked her that same question. Trish would scream at Gina or discipline her if she misbehaved, but she would baby Justin if he misbehaved or did something out of the norm. Sometimes, I think she couldn't stand the sight of Gina, because Gina reminded Trish of herself when she was young.

Gina was everything Trish wasn't. She was innocent. Gina was very friendly with people, strangers especially. Gina was like the daughter I never had. I didn't want to get too attached to Trish's kids because I knew somewhere deep down, I wasn't going to be with Trish forever. If the kids got too attached to me, it would devastate them. I did care about the kids though. You know Vee love the kids.

When me and Trish would be at the apartment, it was only a matter of time before she went ballistic. She needed social media to stay calm, but with social media, she'd easily forget her motherly duties. Once again, I came to Trish's apartment when I got off work, and the apartment was dirty and filthy. We had just had a conversation a week ago about this but I didn't want to say anything bad because she would take it as me being verbally abusive to her. I decided I would rest for a few minutes before I start cleaning the mess myself. I laid on the floor where Trish was, and wrapped my arms around her waist to show her some affection. We hadn't had an argument in a week, ever since she came by my job.

As I was lying down, I felt a slight tingle under my arm pit. I reached under my armpit and pulled out a little white worm from under my arm. I got up off the floor and yelled, "What the fuck? Ooooh my God, noooo!" Trish said, "What's wrong?" I yelled, "Worm!" I looked at Trish and noticed in her braided hair were more worms. I screamed like it was a nightmare. All I kept saying was, "What the fuck? What the fuck?" I ran in the bathroom, turned on the hot water, and poured shampoo all over my body. Trish runs behind me into the bathroom and she starts untangling her hair. I scream at her saying, "Wait, don't come in with me!" She said, "Please Vee, let me get in!" I felt disgusted. Where did they come from? These damn maggots! Eeew!!! You see shit like this on television, but I never thought it would be happening to me.

I had to find out where they came from. The kids were in their room. As I came out of the shower and Trish went in, I went straight to the living room. I noticed the trail of maggots coming from the kitchen. They were coming out of the garbage that had two-week-old rice in it and gnats were flying around it. In the sink, was a pot of one week old rice that was mildewing. It smelled so bad! The only word that came out my mouth was, "Fuck!"

I tried to hold my breath, but the smell won the battle. Trish came out of the shower about fifteen minutes later. She was embarrassed. You could tell from her facial expression. I was upset. I didn't want to say anything that she would take as verbal abuse. I was trying to hold my tongue from saying anything bad, but I just couldn't hold my words back any longer. I said, "Trish, this is nasty as fuck man! How you let this get this bad? You got two kids and you a Haitian woman. How you live like this Trish?" She began to stare off in the distance. Her eyes opened wide and one tear fell from her right eye. She went in the room with the kids for about five minutes. It was a moment of silence. She came back out but didn't say a word to me. She grabbed a broom, bleach, gloves, and started cleaning. I took the garbage out, the whole time wondering how she became so filthy. But then again, Trish was always like that. Ever since she was living in Miami. Ever since the day I met her. I can honestly say, she wasn't the cleanest person I knew.

When I came back in after throwing away the trash, I went to the kitchen to start cleaning the dishes. I saw thongs, grandma panties, and kid's underwear on one side of the sink soaked in a lot of bleach. In the other side, was pots and pans and gnats flying all around because of the pot with the week-old rice in it. I couldn't. I couldn't clean this shit. I told Trish I'd be back. She turned and asked, "Where you going?" I said Rob's house. I left for that whole day and night. I was with Maximus. Trish was blowing my phone up. "Man, fuck that nasty bitch." I wasn't coming to no nasty apartment. Trish was calling nonstop. I finally answered and she asked when was I coming home? I told her, "In an hour," but an hour was a day late.

Trish was highly upset! She was more than mad, but I was disgusted. She felt that I was cheating, seeing someone else, but honestly, I really didn't have the time to cheat on Trish. Although by now, I wanted to start seeing other people. Trish wouldn't go for that. It was her way of living that had me wanting to see other people. Trish would go a day without brushing her teeth and she made it ok for her kids to do the same. When I finally did see Trish, her breath made it hard for me to kiss her.

She'd go a day, sometimes two days, without showering. She usually would shower when she started to feel sticky. What the fuck? She used body spray to try and smell good but Trish was a filthy woman and eventually, I had to say something. If I wanted to have sex with her, she made it hard. She smelled like ass and outdated milk, a complete turn off for me. I thought, maybe she was being filthy on purpose so she wouldn't have sex with me, but this was truly her way of life. I could no longer deal with her filthiness. I tried to end it with Trish by telling her face to face that it was over. It wouldn't be hard at all, or so I thought.

I came in the apartment one night at eleven forty PM and said, "Trish, we need to talk." She was laying on the couch, acting like she was asleep. Her stomach was flat on the sofa, her head on the pillow, but I knew that bitch was wide awake before I came in. Earlier, like ten minutes ago, she was on Facebook putting "lol" and smiley faces on people's Facebook statuses. She didn't realize when she commented on people's pages, it came up on my newsfeed. As soon as I came in the apartment, she wanna play dead? I was sick of her bullshit.

I stood over her stank body by the sofa and said, "Trish, I've been feeling this way for a while and I don't think this is working out. I'm sorry that it's come to this, but this ain't working." Trish slightly opened her eyes and made eye contact. She paused for a few seconds and said, "Hmmm, you ain't going nowhere," and turned her head away from me. I said, "Trish, I think you're not showering on purpose so you don't have to have sex with me. I'm just saying if that's the case, you coulda told me so I wouldn't have to waste my time with you." Then I said in a sarcastic voice, "If you don't want the dick, somebody else will."

Trish turned her head slowly. Her nose flared up. Her eyes opened wide. She got up off the sofa facing me and said, "Alright Vee. You wanna say I stink? You wanna hurt me? Fuck it then!" Trish flipped the coffee table in my direction almost hitting me. I yelled, "You must be crazy flipping that shit near my feet." She jumped off the sofa and said, "What the fuck you gonna do nigga? You ain't gonna do shit!" and grabbed me by my neck. She had both hands around my neck trying to choke me out. My neck was too thick and strong for her to choke me though. I laughed and said, "What you trying to do, tickle me Elmo?" She said, "You think this a game? You ain't going no fucking where bitch!" With the most serious face I've ever seen Trish give me. Something unexplainable mentally had me thinking this was love. I've never had any women I've been with fight to stay together with me. In a weird way, I was turned on by this.

I told Trish, "You gotta start doing better. What you doing is unsanitary. Not bathing and not brushing your teeth, that's nasty." Trish held on to my neck but slowly untightened her grip. Her eyes started to glare as if she was ready to tear up again. I explained to her, "I'm not trying to hurt your feelings or be verbally abusive to you, but how do you tell someone you love that they need to shower without them being sensitive about it?" I told Trish, "You make it hard for me to talk to you." Trish dropped her arms, she let go of my neck, and started to cry. Her shoulders raised up, her head was pointing down, and a river of tears and snot fell from her face onto the floor. She said, "I'm sorry, I was never like that." But

Trish was always like that. She said, "Vee, there are better ways to tell someone they smell." I said "Trish, you got the kids doing the same thing." She replied, "I never do anything right. I'm just an all-around fuck up. Maybe if I died, their lives and your life would be better." Why couldn't she just see my point? Why couldn't she just understand? Maybe I was saying it wrong. Maybe I wasn't clear enough.

I told Trish, "Just make a change, that's all I'm asking." Why didn't I leave? Fuck! This was my chance to leave and I didn't take it. Instead, I gave her another chance. In some form or way, she always manipulated me with her tears and her stories of no one wanting her. Almost to the point where I felt like I had to stay in this relationship to protect her. She put her head on my shoulder and cried. I just stood there with my arms around her. I knew this was getting out of hand between me and Trish, but I was a sucka for a woman in distress. But when I think about it, more like a super save a hoe, as a lot of my friends would say. Me and Trish made up, and she tried to keep clean, but it didn't last long. Once again, it was back to the arguing and threatening and back to more stress.

CHAPTER FIFTEEN
"LIAR LIAR, MARRIAGE ON FIRE"

Trish claimed that she worked at a school for people with disabilities. A new male teacher had arrived to the school and Trish seemed quite fond of her new colleague. Even though she wasn't a teacher, she sure acted like she was one. Christmas was almost here and the teachers and teachers' aides had decided to have Secret Santa gift exchange. That's the game where people get together, pull a name out of a hat, and buy a gift for that person whose name they pulled out. Trish pulled out the new teacher's name and I could tell she was excited about it.

When Trish came home that day, she asked if we could go buy a Christmas gift for her colleague. I asked how much she wanted to spend and she replied, "Does it matter?" I said, "Yes." She started getting really agitated and asked me if she could use my credit card. I told her that I cut up my credit card and only had my debit card now.

She wanted so badly to buy a gift for this man that she had just met. I told her I would get paid in two days, let's just wait until then. She cried out, "Nooo!" I could tell this was no ordinary Christmas gift. She must have made a promise or something. Regardless, I didn't have the money, nor did she, so the gift wasn't purchased. The next morning, Trish got up to leave for work. Something seemed fishy, as if she didn't want to go to work. Trish left that morning. She dropped the kids off to daycare, but she was behind time and late for work. I decided to call Trish at work, not her cell phone, but her actual job's phone. I just had one of those feelings that something was wrong. When I called her job, I told them that I was her fiancé.

The school operator knew Trish well and said, "Oh yes, she just called and said she wasn't coming to work because she was in a car accident." I was concerned and told the operator that I was going to call Trish's cell phone. The operator was nice and asked me to call her back to let her know of Trish's wellbeing. I agreed and called Trish. Trish answered the phone like everything was fine. She said, "Hey". The first thing I thought was this doesn't sound like a woman who's been in an accident.

I was no longer feeling concerned, but curious now. So I played along and said, "Hey Trish." I wanted to see if she was going to tell me that she was really in an accident and where she was, or was she going to lie? I asked, "How's work?" She responded with, "It's good, I'm walking the kids to the playground." All I could think was this bitch is a good ass liar. Why would Trish do this? Why would she lie? Was she seeing someone else? I was so mad that I held the phone up away from my face and started cursing under my breath.

Once I could calm myself down, I let Trish talk, burying herself deeper in her lies. She was good at lying, I see. I had to stop her, because I was hating her more and more as she continued to lie to me. I asked calmly, "Trish, why are you lying? (silence)." This time in a firm voice I said, "Trish, I called your job because I was concerned and wanted to see if you were ok from this morning. They said you called off and that you were in a car accident. First of all, where are you? Are you with someone else? Are you fucking someone else? Tell me the truth, I won't get mad." She began to cry, sobbing over the phone. She cried out, "I'm sorry! I'm not fucking no one I swear on my kids. I'm at the park." "well, you know what Trish, just come home," I told her.

I was done with Trish. I wasn't going to be faithful to her anymore. Since I've been with Trish, I hadn't had sex with anyone else, and I felt stupid for being faithful to someone who has a hoe-ish past. I put on my acting face like I wasn't mad at Trish, but I had some questions for her when she came home. When Trish arrived, she had her head down, still tearing up. She said, "Vee, I'm sorry! Please forgive me." I said, "It's ok Trish, as long as you're ok." I thought she was in a car accident, but now I wish her ass did get into a car accident. I hated Trish's ability to lie so easily, like it came so naturally. She felt she had to bring this new teacher a gift so bad, that she called off of work, losing money and losing my trust. I asked her, "Why was it so important to get this man you just met a gift?" She really couldn't explain, just a lot more of I'm sorries.

I didn't trust Trish any longer. Trish said she needed a therapist to talk to. She needed someone to express her thoughts and feelings to. This bitch got issues and had issues way before I came into the picture. All of a sudden, after I caught her ass, she now wants to seek help? That's some bullshit. After that, me and Trish were never on a good path, but we stayed cordial, for the most part. We weren't happy, but we put up with each other. Trish seemed to need someone to talk to. She lived on her cell phone and on Facebook every day. She was expressing her feelings to random people on social media. I thought to myself, why don't I buy Trish a gift? Maybe that would make her happy. I went to Kays Jewelers that weekend and asked the two older white women working there, "What would be a good gift to make my girl happy?" Both of them said, "Get her a wedding ring!" I said, "Hell naw!" and they both laughed.

The older woman asked, "Is she not worth it?" It was a question that shoulda been easy to answer, but wasn't. I walked around the store for an hour before I made my mind up. I said, "Ladies, let me get a size seven diamond ring and some diamond earrings." They both screamed as if they were gonna be receiving the gifts. The older woman said, "Excellent choice." I had a Kays Jewelers credit card so the price didn't matter to me. They wrapped up the ring and earrings in a nice box. I had thought long and hard on how to make Trish happy and I thought this would work.

To me, this wasn't a wedding ring, it was a gift. A gift I knew Trish was going to love. I called Trish and told her to meet me at the shopping mall. She was at home with the kids. She sounded agitated and upset as always. She gave me excuse after excuse on why she couldn't come. At that point, I felt that I had to lie so Trish would come. The only reason why I wanted her to come, was to get her lazy ass out of the house. Yea, I knew that she was going to be mad, but I was hoping that when she saw the gifts, she would be excited.

I told Trish my car was having problems and I needed her help. She asked me if there was anyone else that I could call? I was getting mad now, like damn, you can't help me?

When she saw that I was getting upset, she inhaled then exhaled, and said in her (I'm annoyed voice), "Alright, I'm coming." When she arrived, she pulled up next to my car with her kids in the back seat. The kids looked like they were sleeping. I got out of my car and opened Trish's driver side door and handed her the gifts. Her eyes lit up, like she was shocked. I was thinking, "Yea bitch, apologize." She slowly opened the box and saw the ring. Her eyes were heavy with tears and she said, "This is the happiest day of my life!" She got out the car and said, "Yes." I asked, "So you like the gift?" She said, "Yes, I have to call my mom and tell her." Trish was so happy. This was my plan and it worked.

As I watched her, I started noticing something. Oh shit, I think Trish thinks that the ring was an engagement ring. Trish was so focused on the ring that she didn't even check for the earrings. I'm not going to lie, it does look like a wedding ring, but it wasn't. To me, it was a promise ring. I know some people might ask, "Why would a grown man give a woman a promise ring? Like we were still in high school." To be honest, at that time, I'd probably say I wasn't mature enough to realize how childish a promise ring was. I mean, it just seemed like a great gift to get her. Was I going to tell Trish that it was just a promise ring after seeing her so happy? Hell no! Let her think that it's an engagement ring. She hasn't been this happy in a while. Why mess that up? I thought. Maybe she would start changing her ways. Cleaning up more around the house and maybe she would even stop lying about certain things.

I really thought this was going to help our relationship in some form of way. After a few hours, Trish went home with the kids. I followed her back to the apartment. My phone started ringing, it was Mason. When I answered, he said, "What the hell is wrong with you?" I said, "What are you talking about?" Mason told me that Trish had posted a wedding ring on Facebook, claiming she was getting married. Mason said, "Tell me this a joke! If it's not, then Vee, you better stop making that hoe feel like she's wifey." I explained to Mason how I had bought her a couple gifts. She was so happy about the ring, she didn't even notice the earrings. Mason said, "If you're not going to marry her, then you need to tell her what the ring really is. Don't let her think it's a wedding ring." She already posted it on Facebook? I thought about saying something, but then decided, fuck it! I'ma just ride it out. He warned me, "Vee, nothing good will come out of this. I keep telling you and you never listen. Just remember I told you." I said, "Ok, I'll talk to you later." I knew Mason was speaking the truth, but like I said, I'm gonna ride this out.

For months, Trish wanted us to set a date for the wedding. She had ordered invitation cards to invite friends and family. She even went as far as getting a wedding dress using her income tax refund check. Oh shit, I thought. This shit was getting too real. I told her, give me a couple of days and let's talk about this together. She was mad. She felt that I was getting cold feet and making up excuses. But it wasn't cold feet. I wasn't marrying no crazy hoe. Sure, I could have just let her go and let some random guy have her, but I was greedy. I was lusting. I didn't want to share Trish with another man. After I told Trish let's wait and talk about it, she fell back into her old habits again. When I came home from work, the house would be dirty. There were dishes that haven't been cleaned for weeks and clothes left on the floor for days. The kids would run and jump in the dirty clothes like it was a bean bag. Even the garbage would stay full.

I realized Trish wasn't the cleanest person in the world, so I didn't too much get upset about it. I knew she was mad and taking it out on me by falling into her old ways, being nasty. Even if marriage played a part in her anger right now, she still would have fell into her old habits of not cleaning. I thought that just giving her the ring would keep her tamed, but instead, it gave her a false hope of marriage. She felt like I lied. I hate to say it, but in a way, I did. I hate to take the responsibility of this, but that's how it played out.

When I laid on the floor watching T.V, Trish would be on the phone with Rawshida. Trish was gossiping about other people's problems. She talked about this one girl that we both knew a lot. Her name was Lorraine. Lorraine was another one of Trish's friends. I wouldn't say they were close because of how bad Trish talked about her to Rawshida.

Lorraine was a very slim, short, black woman who was married, but stepping out on her marriage. Lorraine once confided in Trish about her infidelity. She told Trish that she had met Wender, a long-time crush, at the high school reunion. She had told Trish that she felt guilty for sleeping with Wender after one day of reuniting with him. Lorraine claimed that her and her husband were having a bad marriage, and that's why she slept with Wender. Trish told Rawshida about Lorraine, and said, "Man, that bitch knew exactly what she was doing. She's a hypocrite. One day she's praising the Lord, and the next day, she's sleeping with a bunch of niggas. She ain't just sleep with him one time, but ten more times after that." Trish said, "If it was just one time, I could understand that, but ten times? And then, she got pregnant by him. Not once, but twice!"

I didn't realize Trish was that bad of a gossiper. Trish even told Rawshida that Lorraine had two kids from two different baby daddies'. If Rawshida knew any better, she would be careful telling Trish her problems. Here, I thought

Trish and Lorraine was best friends. When Trish was done talking to Rawshida, I said, "Hey Trish." She said, "What's up?" I sat up so I could see her reaction to what I was going to say. I said, "Trish, I don't think that was cool telling Rawshida about Lorraine's business, especially if she's supposed to be your friend."

When I told Trish that, you can tell she was flaring up. Her eyes got huge, her nostrils opened wider, and not for her to breathe better I'm guessing. She tensed up and said, "Why you listening to my conversation? You act like you like the bitch!?" I looked at Trish in confusion. Like, why she getting so upset? I said, "No boo. I don't like her like that. It's just that when you talk about someone that's supposed to be your friend to someone else, the person you're telling is looking at you in a different light. Like if you can do it to somebody else, you'll do it to them. That's all I'm saying boo." Trish got so mad, she walked out of the apartment.

Marriage was still lingering on her mind, and so anything I said pissed her off. I knew because her eyes said so much. She opened the door and walked out slamming the door behind her. Trish left the kids in the house with me while she was having her temper tantrum. I thought, what the fuck is wrong with this crazy bitch? Naw man, I wasn't going to stick around for this shit. I couldn't marry a woman with this type of behavior. Trish came back home after about twenty-five minutes of walking the neighborhood that day. She walked up towards me and said, "I'm sorry." She said, "I've always had a bad temper. I don't know why or where it came from." As she was telling me this, I wanted to say I know exactly where it comes from. In my opinion, it came from her rough upbringing as a child and the thought of marriage not happening didn't help.

Trish started to cry continuously, with snot all over her face and her eyes flooded with tears. She said, "Vee, please don't leave me! I'm sorry. I'll be a better person, I swear. Just please don't leave us." Her cries were loud. Her kids came out and said, "Mommy, why you cry? Who hurt you?" I wrapped my hands around Trish's waist and said, "I'm here. I'm not going anywhere." I was thinking to myself, Trish went from zero to a hundred in less than a minute. She is very sensitive when you call her out. And she still thinking when is this man gonna give her a wedding date? I realized that I had to be careful with what I say to her.

That following week, Trish received some money from her brother who was in the military. He sent her a little over five hundred dollars. Trish decided to get a tattoo with my name on her right arm. I didn't think she was going to do it, but from what I knew she had tattooed her ex's name on her back shoulder. She covered up his name after they had broken up, so a part of me figured she was serious. We arrived at a tattoo parlor that looked like a hole in the wall. The prices there were affordable. Trish was eager to prove her love to me. She said, "Watch, I'm going to get your name right here on my arm with a butterfly." I wanted to tell her don't tattoo my name. I wanted to stop her, but I also wanted to show that she was my property. You know, like branding a cow.

I said to Trish, "Make sure you add the first letter of my last name at the end, so no one thinks you meant any other Vee out there." She paid for the tattoo. I was surprised and felt a little weird because I never had a woman tattoo my name on their body. I figured, she really does love me if she does it. How can I doubt her now? All my thoughts of me not ever trusting her again had been lifted when she sat down and the needle started going across her arm. She did it, she really did it. Trish had earned a new respect from me when she got the tattoo. A tattoo is forever but I wasn't tattooing her name on me, though. I wanted to show my love for her as well, but I wasn't too fond of needles. I just hope that nothing happens between us, like a breakup. With her temper and ability to lie and my smart mouth, I wondered how long me and Trish were going to last. I wondered... How long?

CHAPTER SIXTEEN
" BEHOLD THE ATTENTION SEEKER"

Trish seemed to be distancing herself away from a lot of her female friends. At least the female friends that were in Miami. Maybe it was something I said? I don't know. I just came from seeing my son and had just left Francis' house. Trish was in the shower after dying her hair red. I had walked in the bathroom while she was naked. Once again, she was reminiscing about her past. Like I said before, she was always talking or thinking about the things that she did and the things that happened to her.

She talked about smoking weed with Julien, the same guy from the reunion who I suspected she was fucking. I had to ask her one more time, "Trish, did you and Julien ever have something going on?" She turned looking at me, then turned away and said, "Yes." "Why did you lie when I asked you the first time?" I asked. She said it was an embarrassing thing to talk about. Apparently, they had been fucking for over six years from what she said. I was blown the fuck away. Wait, so that means while she was in other relationships, she was cheating on her partners with Julien? I was curious, "Were you in relationships at the time?" She paused and then said, "No." She claims that when she'd have an argument with her partners, she would need a fix, something like a sex reliever. She tried to make it seem like she wasn't in a relationship when she was fucking him, but the timeline didn't add up. She was lying, I knew already.

I said, "Trish, how did it happen? How did it start?" She said her dad used to give her an allowance of a hundred dollars a week. Julien use to con her into giving him money when she first came to North Miami. She thought she could keep friends by buying them weed and giving them money. One day, he persuaded her to come to his house. Trish had studied him and knew his likes and dislikes. She knew he had a passion for music, especially Tupac. She then studied every piece of music from Tupac. While they were at his house, she rapped a few songs from Tupac's album. Julien was impressed and got straight to the point. He asked her, "Do you want to fuck?" Easily, she replied, "Yea." And ever since then, they've been fucking. I asked her why they hadn't become a couple. She explained that she had asked him, but his response was, "Because of your past, I can't fuck with you like that." She told him that she understands, but she was hurt. She said, "Vee, when Julien told me that, I didn't think I would ever find someone like you to love me." Even though Trish tried to butter me up with that last line, the only thing going through my mind was, "What else is this bitch lying about?"

"Trish, have you ever caught any sexually transmitted diseases?" She said, "Yes..." Before she could even finish her sentence, I started drilling her about who she got it from and exactly what diseases she had gotten? "Syphilis, chlamydia, and HPV" she said. "One was by a guy she met on tag, an internet dating site, and the other time was by her baby daddy." She even told me that he had been arrested several times for soliciting sex from transvestite prostitutes. He was once caught receiving a blow job from a trani. Her baby daddy was never treated for the STD's. After that, he had sex with Trish and gave it to her. There were so many questions I wanted to ask Trish. The story just didn't make sense. So, you found out your baby daddy was arrested for getting his dick sucked by a trani. Wouldn't you be mad? At least, wouldn't you make him take an STD test? Why have sex with him?

Trish is so easily tempered, that if I started asking her for specific dates and times, it woulda been a problem. She claims she was treated for syphilis and HPV at a local clinic. She had caught chlamydia after a brief encounter with a younger guy she met on the tag website. The dating site where women and men chat on line and hook up, basically. At this time, Trish had already had her kids and was staying with her baby daddy. She'd leave her kids sometimes with her sister or their dad and go and meet up with this guy that she'd met on line. Trish hardly knew the guy. Barely knew his name, but wanted true love. This guy just wanted to fuck, simple as that. There were no flowers, dinner, or a first date to the movies. One day, they had unprotective sex and Trish noticed a burning sensation in her vagina when she peed. She knew what it was because she'd had an STD before. She called the guy on his cell phone, he never answered. She even went to his house. He had moved away to Atlanta, from what his parents said. She was so mad, that she cursed his parents out and made threats that she would kill him if she ever saw him again. She even went as far as copying and pasting his picture on the tag website and defaming his character. After that, she did the same thing on social media, telling the world that he had AIDS.

This was her way of revenge. I thought, I better not piss this bitch off. Trish slipped and told me that she had given Julien chlamydia while having sex with him and two other guys in the same time frame. I was stunned. Once again, she lied to me. So it wasn't just the guy from tag that she was fucking, she was fucking two other guys as well without a condom. Oh shit, I thought, she must have a death wish fucking these guys unprotected. In a shocking tone, I asked, "So you were fucking Julien, the guy from tag, and your baby daddy?" She replied, "No, not like that." As if she was worried that I would judge her, too late! She said, "Vee, now you trying to make me sound like a hoe." I said, "Trish, that's your past, but if you wanna talk about it, let's talk. But if not, fuck it." She said she didn't like my facial expressions or my tone of voice when I responded to her. I told her I didn't know I was making faces. Trish said I was making a disgusted face.

Maybe I was, but I believe she was in her feelings, very sensitive. I told her, "I'm sorry, and I'll try not to do any faces." She continued her story but appeared to be embarrassed now. I asked, "Did you know you had it when you gave it to Julien?" She would not answer. I asked again, "Trish, did you know? She yelled, "Vee!" in a frustrating voice, "I can hear you and no, I didn't know I had it." Damn, Trish was a liar, but I wasn't going to say anything. I walked out of the bathroom, scared that I might've caught something from her. I thought, what am I doing with Trish? How far is this relationship going to go? From what I knew and now know about her, she has a lot of issues and all of them surrounded by men. She wouldn't be a faithful woman to me. I know that I'm no saint. I have some skeletons in my closet as well, but not a bad as Trish. She was a strong woman, but she would never truly be a good woman. In my opinion, because she wouldn't let go of her past and her excessive fabrications of the truth, this would be the down fall for our future relationship.

I decided, as I was going to work at the shopping mall that next day, me and Trish's relationship was doomed to fail. She never got the help she needed for all her issues and I knew this relationship would never work the way she wanted it to. While at work, around three PM, Trish called my cell phone. I answered, "Hello" and she said, "What's up?" It was displeasing the way she said it, like she was really saying, "Whatever" disrespectfully. I asked, "What's up Trish?" She didn't say much, but answered me with short words and phrases. I said, "Trish, you know we have been having a lot of problems, and it seems to be getting worse. I just think we need to split up for a while."

She was silent. All I could hear was her breathing in the background. I said, "Hello?" I was sure she had hung up on me, but I was wrong. She said, "You know what Vee, you brought me and my kids out here just so you can leave us? Naw nigga, you got the right bitch!" I had to remind her, "Trish, you the one who begged me to get you and your kids out here! Don't you remember? You said you would die in Miami! You said that I helped you and your kids. I still haven't gotten my thank you, Vee, for saving your ungrateful ass!" Trish screamed, "Fuck you! God as my witness Vee, you will pay." I said, "Trish, why make threats you can't keep? Let's just end this and be friends." "I moved up here for you," Trish said. I yelled, holding my phone tight, "Oh hell no you didn't! You moved up here to make a better life for your kids."

I could hear a door slam in the background, and Trish telling her kids hurry up and get in. She said, "Vee, I'm tired. I'm so tired. My life would be so much better if I just ended my life." I rolled my eyes in disbelief, "Trish really? Now you sound crazy. I don't think you're able to do some shit like that. Trish, you are too strong of a woman. I don't believe you." I'm not a counselor, I'm not a therapist, and I'm not a negotiator. I've never dealt with anything like this. She said, "Watch Vee. I'm gonna do it and tell all my family it was because of you." I started laughing, what else was I supposed to do? This was unreal for me.

I said, "Trish, how you gonna tell your family it's because of me if you already killed yourself? If you kill yourself first, they wouldn't know." I said all these things not knowing that I had now given her the idea to make a video blaming me for her suicide. She said, "I'm gonna email them all and say it was because of you. You dumb ass!" I replied sarcastically, "Ok Trish, now we gonna resort to name calling? Alright Trish, have a nice day." I hung the phone up and seconds later, she was calling me back. I thought to myself, why entertain Trish? She called over twenty-eight times and then started texting me uncontrollably. I figured the best thing to do is just turn my cell phone off. Suddenly, my job phone started ringing. All I was saying to myself is, that it better not be Trish. I looked at the caller ID, it was a four zero seven number. I answered, "Security, may I help you?" I heard Trish's voice, "You can't get rid of me, fuck nigga! Trust that." I said, "Is this you, Trish?" she replied, "Fuck you! You know it's me."

Trish was going to get me fired by her actions, and I wasn't going to lose this job because of her stupidity. I said, "Trish, don't call my job phone anymore." She said, "then turn your phone on." I felt like a hostage trapped in my own spider web that I created. "Ok," I told her and turned my phone back on. This was some crazy shit Trish was doing. A thin line between love and hate crazy shit. Did I like it? Yes and no. Yes, because it showed me that she cared enough to at least fight for us to be together. But no, because now she was interfering with my job. As soon as I turned my cell phone on, Trish called and all her texts flooded my cell phone. She said, "Vee, I have a knife and I'm ready. But you don't care." While she was saying that, I wondered where the kids were, but I didn't ask. I said, "Trish, I care but I know you're just doing this for attention." She said, "Check your texts. I looked at my texts. She had sent me a picture of a knife to her wrist.

Oh my God, she is really gonna do it, I thought. What was I supposed to think? I've never been in this type of situation before. I have never had anyone tell me that they were gonna commit suicide and actually had the means to do it. I said, "Trish, what are you doing?" She replied, "Does it look like I'm playing fucking games now? Vee, I just want you to make sure my kids get the insurance money." I said, "Trish, wait, is this really necessary? Let's talk about this." She yelled, "No! Fuck it! I'm sick and tired of talking about it. I'm a bad mother, I'm a hoe, my father hates me, and my mom thinks I'm a failure. It would be better for everyone if I was just dead." I tried to talk Trish out of doing whatever she was planning. She yelled, "No, no, no! I'm just fucking done with this life. Can you make sure Victor don't get my kids?" I said, "Who?" she repeated, "Victor, my kids' father." This was the first time I'd ever heard her say his name since I've been with Trish. "Don't let him get my kids Vee. He won't raise them right with his drinking problem." She's saying he can't take care of the kids right because of his drinking problem, but she's the one trying to kill herself, possibly in front of the kids?

I couldn't tell Trish that, so I just said, "Trish, if you don't want him to have the kids, then don't do whatever you're planning." She yelled, "Fuck my life!" and the phone went silent. She had hung up on me. I held my phone saying, "Hello?" for a whole minute. I thought, what should I do? Should I call back, call 911, or just ignore her? She just probably needed some attention. After five minutes of thinking, I called Trish. She didn't answer. I kept calling, no answer. I called my cousin, Shelly, who lived around the corner from Trish. I wanted to see if she could check on Trish. Shelly never answered. I was concerned. I started thinking, Trish probably did do it. Damn, she probably did it. Oh man, should I leave work? What if this was one of her attention seeking moments? I didn't want to leave work because she could just be crying out for attention.

I decided to call the city police and have them check out the apartment. I didn't want to tell them that Trish had threatened to kill herself and sent me a picture of a knife to her wrist. I informed the operator that the last thing I heard was a loud scream and the phone went dead. The operator said she was sending a unit out there, and that she would call me back to inform me of what was going on. I waited for thirty to forty minutes. I then received a call from Trish's cell phone. I answered quickly, saying, "Hello?" in a concerned tone of voice. I could hear voices. Trish's voice and a man's voice. I don't know who called me, but I was guessing it was Trish. Maybe it was by accident, I thought.

I could hear Trish yelling at someone, "My kids haven't eaten all day! I'm just getting them a banana." The man says, "Ma'am, come out of the kitchen now! They can wait a few more minutes." I now realized that the man that was talking to Trish, was a cop. Trish was yelling at the cop, telling him everything is fine and you can leave now. The cop said, "We received a call and we will not leave until we make sure everyone is fine." He repeatedly asked Trish to step into the living room but she continued saying, "My kids haven't eaten, I'm getting them snacks." I hear the cop say, "I don't know if you're getting a knife or any kind of weapon, so I'm asking one last time, step in the living room." Trish was defiant. She replied, "Once again, I'm getting my kids..." (noises) And then I heard a struggle. Trish was yelling, "What the fuck? I was just getting my kids a snack! Fuck! What are you doing?! You're hurting me, let me go! Is this how you handle women?!! Aw shit, you're fucking hurting me!!" I could hear the cop say, "If only you'd complied." The last words I heard Trish say was, "Shit, Goddamn it!!!" And then her voice faded.

In the background, you could hear the kids scream, "Mommy! Where you taking mommy?" I seriously couldn't believe my ears. I was screaming, "Hello! Helloooo!!" What the fuck just happened? I then heard heavy breathing as if someone was listening. I knew it wasn't the kids because it sounded like a manly, heavy, breathing. Like someone who had just ran a marathon. The phone went silent. Shit was getting real confusing. I called the operator, "What's going on at my apartment? I sent cops out there to check on my girlfriend and now she's getting arrested?" The operator said, "Let me see what's going on and I will let you know. One second."

The operator put me on hold. It felt like forever, but after two minutes, she said she would have the officer call me. I gave her my number and in just ten minutes, the officer called me. He identified himself as officer Daniel. He was trying to be professional. He explained that when he arrived at the apartment, he made contact with the female. When she opened the door, she opened it with a force. The officer then said that when he looked in the apartment, he saw a kitchen knife that was on the floor. He asked Trish could they come in to talk privately. Trish replied loudly, "Ain't nothing here! I know my rights; my kids are fine. Ya can goooo!"

He said he told Trish that he was concerned for the safety of the kids and he received a call about a woman screaming. All he wanted to do was see if everyone in the apartment was fine. Trish then allowed them in, yelling, "Come in then! Ya see ain't nothing wrong. Now get out!" In a rude manner. Trish was tempered from what the officer explained. Knowing Trish, I can imagine that.

He said she then speed walked straight towards the kitchen and was in the kitchen sink for over three to four minutes. He couldn't see what Trish was doing and thought she was grabbing a weapon. He asked her to get out of the kitchen more than several times, she refused all commands. He then said he tried to escort her out the kitchen by placing his hand on her elbow. She then elbowed him in the chest. He said from there, it was a tuffling match. She yelled, screamed, cursed, and put up a fight which is what got her in cuffs. After he got her outside to his car, she refused to go into the police car. She kicked and dropped herself to the floor until he pulled out his taser. He said that once she saw the taser, she immediately got up and said, "Ok, ok I'll go in the car."

The officer even said that Trish would not give them her name. He went back in the house to find any form of paperwork with her name on it, but what they came across was a prelude suicide letter. The letter stated, "In this life, we make mistakes. I am not a good mother. I leave my son for my father to take care of and my daughter, for my mom to take care of. I am sorry for all that I have put everyone through." The letter was not finished, as if the officer had interrupted her from finishing the letter. Wow, Trish was really gonna go through with this. I couldn't believe it. The officer asked me, "How long will it take for you to come to the apartment? I told him, "I'm at work and it's gonna take a while to find someone to cover for me at this time." He told me that his partner was with the kids and he would appreciate if I got here as soon as possible. I said, "Ok." He then asked me for Trish's real name. I froze. If Trish didn't give him her name, why should I? I pretended that my phone was acting up and hung up. He called back, but I didn't answer. He left a voice message saying that he was trying to be nice, but if I didn't get there to the apartment, he was going to have child services come and get Trish's kids.

I now had to make a decision, whether to leave my job unattended and possibly get fired, or find someone to cover me or work for me. A couple hours had passed, it was now seven o'clock. I had called my supervisor explaining that I had a family emergency, and if there was some way he could get someone to work my zone for now? He was a little upset and said, "Vee, this is short notice, but I'll try to find someone," and then hung up on me. He was not happy.

Fifteen minutes later, the supervisor said he was on his way. It took him forty minutes to get there, but the sooner the better. I passed on the keys and radio and rushed over to Trish's apartment. When I got there, there was still one officer outside the apartment. The kids were inside watching Scooby Doo. I walked up towards the apartment and the officer greeted me. He introduced himself as officer Santiago. I said, "You're not the same guy that I was talking to?" He said, "No, that was my partner." Officer Santiago informed me of the same story that officer Daniel had told me and said that Trish was easily tempered. He told me how she slammed the door open against the wall and that they had found a suicide letter near the knife that was on the floor. Officer Santiago showed me the letter. I was shocked and in disbelief. Was it that serious of a problem that Trish was willing to take her own life?

As me and officer Santiago talked, a car pulled up. It was a woman from child services. Oh shit, Officer Daniel did call child services. I can't say I'm surprised though. The child services worker introduced herself as Mona. Officer Santiago explained to Mona the situation. Mona wanted to see the kids. Mind you, I hadn't walked in the apartment yet. When officer Santiago, Mona, and I walked into the apartment, it was filthy. Oh my God, I was so embarrassed. Mona asked, "Is the house always this dirty?" I lied and said, "No." There were clothes, paper, and garbage all over the living room. Damn, the bed room had clothes all over the floor and the closet was stacked up high with about two feet of clothes too. The only spot in the entire place that was clean was the bathroom. The kids ran to me, both telling me, "Vee, police take mommy."

Mona looked at the kids and looked in the fridge. Mona said, "These kids can't stay here." My mouth dropped. She asked, "Is there a relative that can come get them?" I said their father is in Miami. She asked, "Well, what about anyone else?" I was confused, "Why can't they stay with me?" She replied, "Since you're not their biological dad, we would need Trish's permission." Officer Santiago radioed officer Daniel to ask Trish if she would allow the kids to stay with me and she gave them permission. Mona told me that the kids still needed to get out of the apartment until someone cleaned it up. She felt that they can't and shouldn't live like this.

I found Trish's phone in the kitchen and looked up her brother. While looking for her brother's number, a text came in from some guy in Orlando saying, "What's up sexy?" I wanted to make sure I wasn't seeing things, so I replied, "What's up boo?", pretending to be Trish. The guy texted back, "Let me know when you're free." I stopped looking for Trish's brother and started looking through her texts. She's been talking to this guy for a while now, telling him she's an aggressive woman. She also told him things like, "She always gets what she wants." I was hurt, and here she was acting like she was going to kill herself for the sake of love. Bitch, die!

Mona saw me on the cell phone and said, "Are you calling someone?" I said, "Yes, Trish's brother." Mona said, "Oh yes, I would like to talk to him." I found Trish's brother's number and called him. He answered. This was really the first time we had ever spoken since me and Trish have been together. I told him who I was and what was going on. He sounded as if he wanted to cry, but was holding it in. This was the brother who was in the military. Mona wanted to talk to him. She asked him about Trish's life with her parents and her growing up. Trish's brother said, "She had a rough life and she didn't get along with her dad. He wasn't abusive, he was just strict." After the talk with Mona, Trish's brother offered to come, but I told him I would take care of it. After the police left, I was trying to find a place where the kids could stay. Mona was not leaving until I found some place that was clean.

I walked over to my cousin Shelly's apartment with the kids and Mona. Shelly answered the door. I said, "Cuz, I've been trying to call you all day! Where have you been?" She said that her phone wasn't working. I explained the situation to her and she allowed Mona to look at her apartment to approve of the kids staying there. Mona said, "Yes, they can stay here," and she left. I told my cousin to watch the kids so that I could clean the apartment. She agreed but made sure to say, "Vee, I told you no good would come out of this. God has a plan for you and this is one of his ways of telling you, this isn't good." I said, "Ok cuz," ignoring her words. "I'll be back."

CHAPTER SEVENTEEN
"THE BREAK DOWN"

I went back to Trish's apartment to clean it up. I stood inside and looked around. The apartment was so filthy. I couldn't believe that any woman could live this way. There was even leftover food under the kids' bed. It was a mess. I stayed there cleaning up Trish's apartment for over three hours. After seeing the text on Trish's phone from that guy in Orlando, I thought, "Let that bitch rot in jail." It hurt cleaning Trish's apartment, knowing she was seeing someone else, but I felt obligated to do it for the kids. It was late now, about three in the morning. I kept looking online on Trish's laptop to see if she had been booked into the county jail yet. Trish still hadn't been booked. Everything felt unreal, like it was a movie. I was so tired. I took a shower after I cleaned up.

I looked online again to see if Trish was booked. Finally, she was booked at six in the morning. Her bond was set at $2000. I texted her brother to inform him of how much the bond was. He texted back and said it didn't matter how much, he would pay for it. In about an hour, he sent the money to me through western union. I went to my cousin's apartment and got Trish's kids ready for day care. Once the kids were dressed, I dropped them off. I then went to the county book-in area, where I paid for Trish's bond. The cashier informed me that Trish would be out in six hours. Shocked, I asked, "Why so long?" She said they had already transferred her to Frost Proof, another in Polk County. I waited five hours, then drove across the street to the sub shop for a drink. While at the sub shop, I thought, what will I say to Trish when I see her? What will she say to me? So many thoughts were running through my mind.

I drove back and as I pulled up, Trish was outside in front of the jail still in her work clothes that she had on when she was arrested. Her hair was a mess. No makeup on her face, just raw blemishes. She looked so emotionally drained. I pulled up in my car in front of the building. I was getting ready to get out of the car to embrace Trish, but she opened my passenger door herself and quickly sat down. She leaped over the hand rest and hugged me, and I hugged her. She began to cry a river of tears. My heart felt some type of way. It was like a tingling feeling. After she hugged me, she said, "I'm sorry." I said, "Trish, you don't have to apologize." She cried out, "It's my fault!" I paused and asked, "What do you mean?" She said everything is my fault, "I'm just a fuck up! Why God? Why me?", and cried uncontrollably.

I waited for Trish to calm down. She was having a meltdown. I pulled over and tried to comfort her, "Trish, it's ok. It's not your fault." Twenty minutes had passed and it was already time to pick up Trish's kids. I gave her a kiss on her lips, and assured her that everything would be fine. She looked in my eyes and nodded her head as acknowledgement. Once I saw that she was ok, I began driving to pick her kids up from daycare.

On the ride to pick the kids up, she spoke about how horrible jail was. Her first day in jail, she cried, "Help!" The correctional officers told her to shut the fuck up. Trish felt powerless and weak, like no one could hear her cries for help. Trish also said that she was forced to strip naked in front of male employees, staring at her naked body. Trish was put under suicide watch while in jail. After she was stripped naked, she was given a white gown to wear so she couldn't harm herself. Normally, inmates wear the orange pants and white t-shirt with an ID tag so they can be identified easier. Those who are on suicide watch, must wear the white gown and without tags.

She said she was treated like an animal. She told me how the other inmates were screaming at her and saying things like they were going to rape her later. Trish got sick while in jail. She contracted strep throat. It was getting bad because her voice sounded extra raspy. At this point, she was just glad to be out of there. I finally got to the daycare and pulled up in front of the school. Trish stayed in the car because of her appearance and smell. It wasn't until she mentioned her body odor that I realized how bad she smelled. She didn't have time to bathe nor did she brush her teeth.

I told Trish, "Let me get the kids and you'll surprise them." When I went in and brought the kids out, they were asking me, "Where's mommy? Is mommy coming back?" I told the kids, "Mommy is ok." And Trish got out of the car crying with her arms opened. The kids ran towards Trish screaming, "Mommy! Mommy!" It was an emotional moment to see them back together again. Trish held her kids tight for two minutes. Justin said, "Mommy, why police take you mommy?" I ain't gonna lie, it sent a chill down to my heart. I think it was the way he looked at his mom for an answer, but only saw tears from her eyes. Her daughter didn't say much, just giggled and said, "I miss you mommy."

Trish and the kids got in the car. They all seemed so happy and overjoyed. When we got to the apartment, Trish went to the spot where she was taken down by officer Daniel, and started crying. I told Trish about child services. I only explained that child services came and said that the house should remain clean and livable for the kids. Trish's breathing got heavy when I spoke about child services. The apartment was spotless, clean as a whistle, I would say. The kids ran in their room, just happy to be home.

I fixed Trish a warm bubble bath. I didn't want to bring up any drama right now, maybe a little later. Trish took her clothes off. Damn she smelled bad! She sat in the tub and cried again. I scrubbed her back and said, "Everything will be alright." Scrubbing her back and watching the dirt come off her skin was like watching mud fall off a pig. At least it was a pig I was willing to clean, even after the texts I saw on her phone. When Trish was done bathing, I got her clothes and fixed her and the kids dinner. More like I ordered pizza. The kids ate like they hadn't eaten in years and Trish cried in the kid's room. It was gonna take some time before she could stop. I gave her some space and tended to the kids.

Trish's mom, her brothers, and sister called. They were asking questions and Trish didn't want to talk anymore. She didn't know what to say to anyone who asked what happened. When it got dark, I put the kids to sleep. Trish was in the living room, still up. I sat next to her and said, "Do you want to talk?" She didn't say yes or no. She began by saying, "My life is over, why is God punishing me?" She continued, "I think God is punishing me for all the things I've done in my past." It was as if Trish was looking for someone to blame. She vented and vented until one point, she went so far to say that someone must have put voodoo on her. Trish was upset with her own life and with the direction she had taken it.

I asked Trish what happened when the police came to the house? She explained to me that officer Daniel was really rough with her. I asked Trish, "Did you allow them in the apartment?" She answered, "Yes, but only because officer Daniel said he wouldn't leave until he came in." I advised Trish, "Don't say or tell anyone that you allowed them in. That will get you into deeper problems." I wanted to know what else had happened when they came in? She said, "I don't know, I can't remember." "Trish, it just happened, how can you forget? It was only yesterday," I asked. Trish cried out, "I don't know! I can't remember!" and started crying again. Honestly, I think she didn't want to remember.

I knew Trish well enough to know that she remembered, just refused to talk about it. I left the conversation alone because it seemed too much for Trish. I told Trish I had to go to work, but really, I was going to Francis' house to see Maximus. She wanted me to call off work, but I felt like I was neglecting my son, Maximus. I was spending all this time with Trish and her kids. Trish didn't want me to leave. She was giving me the puppy eyes. I told her I would stay for a while, but I would have to call my job and tell them I'm coming in late. I pretended to call my job, but I called Mason. I walked out the apartment to talk to Mason. He was surprised that I called him. It had been a while since I had spoken to him. That was only because I didn't want him knowing what was going on between me and Trish. As we talked, I told him about her trying to commit suicide. "Vee, leave her now! Don't stay with someone like that. She's going to take you down with her if you don't leave, just watch," he warned.

Damn, Mason's words cut me mentally, because in a way, I knew he was right. Trish opened the apartment door and asked, "Why do you have to talk outside?" I told Trish to give me a minute. Mason heard her in the background and said, "Man, you digging your own grave. I've already told you." I told him I would call him back. He said, "I hope you hear my words." and hung up.

Trish stood by the door waiting for me to tell her who I was talking to. When I didn't tell her, she asked in a curious tone of voice, "Who was that you was talking to so privately?" I said, "Trish, I told you already I was calling my job. Do you need something?" she said, "No." I told Trish to not worry and that everything was going to be fine. When I left, she seemed scared to be alone. She called me every thirty minutes and wouldn't say much on the phone. When I got to Francis' house, I was tired. All the excitement that was going on with Trish had me drained.

Francis was sitting in the living room laying on the couch. She had on the same clothes that she usually wears when she's off work. The old grandma long pants and the seventies white tee shirt. Francis was so predictable. She was watching the oxygen channel and Maximus was sleeping. Francis said, "Where you been? Your hoes got you on mission impossible?" She was indirect in what she really wanted to say. I didn't respond to Francis because I knew that's exactly what she was looking for.

I went into Maximus' room and saw that he was sleeping. Francis had a queen size bed where Maximus slept. I was so tired, I decided to sleep right next to him. Soon, I was knocked out. I woke up to find that I had slept all night until early morning. It was now eight in the morning. Maximus was gone and so was Francis. I took my phone out of my pocket and saw I had almost forty missed calls from Trish. I called Francis. She answered saying she was at work and that she had dropped Maximus off to daycare. She didn't want to wake me up since I was snoring like a baby. I told her, "Thanks a lot."

Francis wanted to know if I could pick Maximus up from daycare that afternoon? I told her, "Yes, it's not a problem." She seemed as if she was using Maximus to get me to come home. She said, "Please take him to the park and do not feed him hamburgers." I told her, "Ok, I understand. I'm not dumb." She hung up and I got up to shower and brush my teeth, pretty much freshen up.

I called Trish. When she answered, she was asking questions like a drill sergeant. "Where you at? Who you with? Why did it take you so long to call me back?" I said, "Trish, I told you I was at work." She told me the kids needed to go to daycare and that it was my fault they didn't go. I asked, "Why are you blaming me? Don't you have a car? Can't you drive?" She replied, "Yea, but Vee, you know what I've been through. I needed you to do that." I said, "Trish, you ain't tell me nothing! How am I supposed to know?" She yells, "If you answered your phone, you would know!"

Here we go again I thought. Her temper was getting out of control. Can't say I understand how she feels because I've never been arrested. After I had freshened up, I went to Trish's apartment. She was laying on the sofa bed. She didn't even take a shower or brush her teeth. She was far from ready. The kids weren't ready either. They were watching TV and still had on the same clothes from yesterday. I said, "Trish, obviously, the kids and you are not ready." Nothing. Trish was texting. It almost felt like she was ignoring me. I yelled, "Trish! Do you hear me?" She turned her head in my direction and gave me an angry look. I said, "Trish, isn't it too late to bring the kids to day care?" She said, "No." and yelled for the kids to put their clothes on.

The kids hadn't even showered. Damn, if I say something, she will get hot tempered. Fuck it, I went to the kids made them brush their teeth and wash their faces for now. Shit, they weren't my kids, but I treated them as if they were. Her son Justin was a trouble maker, already fighting with his sister to brush his teeth first. I said, "Justin, be nice to your sister." And he pushes her on the floor. I know Justin has a special problem, but he was also violent. I yelled for Trish to come to the bathroom. She walked in slow paced. When she got there, she said, "What!" like I was disturbing her from doing nothing. I told her that Justin had pushed Gina down. Trish didn't even let me finish the whole sentence and started hitting Justin. She said, "You just like your daddy," and gave him a slap on the head." Trish looked at me and asked, "Are they done?" When I told her no, she said, "Just take them now." And walked back to her sofa.

I told the kids to go put on their clothes. Gina went but Justin started walking slowly, then stopped. He turned around at my direction and said, "Vee, you not my friend anymore," then ran into his room. That big head kid never talked, only when he wanted some cookies. When he finally did talk, that's what he says? Oh well, like I said before, that ain't my kid. Big head punk. When the kids got their clothes ready, I told Trish that I would be back. As she laid on that sofa still texting, she mumbled, "Yea, ok." After taking the kids to school, I thought, Trish was just feeling depressed from the arrest. It'll get better soon, I hope. This went on for a week. Trish didn't bathe and she was causing the apartment to have a stench, a smell that wasn't pleasant. She didn't brush her teeth, nor was she making food for the kids. I thought as always, I should say something, but I was going to come at her with a different angle only because of Trish's temper. It might come off rude, me telling or asking her to clean herself up.

I sat down near Trish one Friday afternoon. I said, "Honey, let's take a shower." She said she wasn't ready. When she said that, I knew I had to say something now or never. I said, "Trish, you haven't showered in a week or even brushed your teeth. This isn't healthy for you. I'm worried about you Trish." Before I could finish, she got up and went to the bathroom. Damn, did I say something wrong? I heard the water in the shower turn on. I guess I said something right. Trish left her phone on the sofa. It was vibrating as if someone had texted her. I picked it up and saw it was her guy friend from Orlando. "It's going to be ok, the police ain't had no rights to come in your apartment," he texted. I think it was time to bring this shit up to Trish. I sacrificed a lot to be with someone who everyone told me was a hoe. She was very promiscuous. I didn't listen, but now that I see all the signs, it was clear. Trish didn't need me. I was just convenient for her and her kids. We hadn't had sex in a while, and the last time we did, her style of sucking my dick had changed. That's when I knew something was different. Either way, I had to get to the bottom of it.

When Trish was done showering, I asked Trish, "Do you blame me for what happened to you?" The only reason why I asked that was because of her attitude towards me lately. She stayed silent as if she wanted to say yes. I said, "Damn, I know you heard me Trish." I asked again, "Do you blame me for you getting arrested?" She yelled out, "You don't know when a bitch trying to get some attention from you!

Instead, you called the police. You fuckin snitch!" I froze. Now the truth comes out on how she really feels. I said to Trish, "You know what, you a crazy bitch. I ain't never had no one send me a picture with a knife to their wrist or ever had anyone talk about killing themselves. You act like that shit is normal. Maybe I shoulda let you do it and not called the police. Maybe I shouldn't care so fucking much! Why don't you go do that shit with that nigga from Orlando? He might know how to deal with crazy bitches like you."

Trish grabs a handful of plates and started throwing them against the wall. She yells out, "Fuck you!!" She was getting so loud in the apartment, I thought the police were going to get called on us. I yelled out, "So you not denying ya nigga in Orlando?" Instead of answering the question, Trish asked, "You been going through my phone?" I said, "So you admit you fucking another nigga. Damn, I shoulda listened when them boys said you ain't nothing but a hoe." I said that purposely to upset her even more. I was pissed and didn't care about her feelings anymore.

Trish threw a plate in my direction. I ducked and yelled, "Bitch, if that shit woulda hit me...!" Trish says to me, "You ain't gonna do shit, bitch ass nigga." I had enough. I told Trish, "Have that nigga pay for the rent, you crazy bitch. I'm out!" She runs and pushes me away from the door and says in a demonic voice, "You're not going anywhere." When she pushed me, I thought, "Oh shit, what the fuck am I going to do?" I said, "Trish, I'm not trying to fight with you, let me just go take a walk." She yells out, "No! I'm tired of you always saying you leaving me. You gonna sit the fuck down and talk!" Her eyes were open wide and she was looking like she was in fight mode.

I stood up and said, "Trish, get out my fucking way!" I

grabbed the door handle. Trish grabbed my neck with her left hand and began putting pressure on it. "Bitch, you didn't hear what I said?" She asked. It was like time had stopped for me. This bitch just grabbed me. Not only did she grab me, but she's putting pressure on my neck. Oh, hell now! I grabbed her wrist and pulled her hand away from my neck. It wasn't easy pulling her hands off my neck though. With my hand around her wrist, I finally got her down to the ground.

As Trish was on the floor, I unlocked the door and started to open it. She kicked it closed, almost closing the door on my fingers. "What the fuck!", I yelled out loud. "What the fuck do you want from me?" Trish grabbed my leg and wrestled me down. Oh shit! This bitch actually took me down. As crazy as it sounds, it was kind of sexy. My butt hit the floor hard. Trish grabbed me by my neck again and says, "You gonna listen to me, bitch!" I could have easily flipped Trish on her back or even held her down. But for her to take me down like she did, I guess I'd listen and hear what this bitch had to say. I said, "If you want me to listen, I suggest you get your hand off my neck." Trish was breathing heavy like a wild animal. She slowly took her hands off and away from my neck. She was between my legs, mostly on top of me.

I knew Trish was a little off, but for her to become so aggressive and violent, it showed me that there was more to Trish than what she appeared to be. I said, "So tell me, are you fucking this guy from Orlando?" Trish says, "No, he's just my friend. He's like my big brother and I always go to him for advice." I asked, "Do you talk to him about our relationship?" She paused and said, "Yes." I was surprised that she was able to tell the truth. "Trish," I said. "I'm a man. No man likes his woman telling another man about their business. How would you like it if I did that to you?" Trish was silent. I said, "Trish, the way he's talking to you sounds like you and him had fucked and still fucking now." She said, "No, we are not having sex." I asked, "Trish, have you ever had sex with him since you known him? She yells, "What does my past have to do with now?"

For her not to answer the question and instead ask what her past had to do with now, I was convinced that they had fucked before. I yell, "What the fuck?" in disappointment. She yells out, "It was only once, a long time ago when I was eighteen." I said, "Trish, do you keep in contact with every guy you've had sex with? And the bad part about it is that you're calling him your big brother." She looked confused, like she didn't see anything wrong with being friends with guys she'd had sex with. It might look like I was insecure, but I had a good reason. My thought of this situation was clear. This nigga was in the friend zone until me and Trish would break up. Then, he would make his move on her. He had a dick and Trish had a pussy. He knew of her past and I'm guessing he wanted to fuck. Or, he was already fucking her.

She looked so dumbfounded. I wanted to ask her how could she be so gullible. Only if I had done her the same way, she'd understand. But I know she didn't understand because she kept trying to justify her actions. She said she never did anything with this guy while we were together. She even swore on her kids' life, but I was done trusting Trish. I had enough of her lies. I know I've said it plenty of times before, but this time was different. It was different because I hated her. She listened to every word her male friends said and didn't respect my opinion. I saw how the things he said encouraged her, the way I used to. I couldn't be mad with him because he was just being a typical man in the friend zone. But Trish, she was playing me even after all I did for her. I got up off of the floor. Trish took her phone and texted him in front of me, telling him that they could no longer be friends. He responded with a text back, "Ok."

Even though Trish did that in front of me, I still didn't trust her. She yelled, "You see? I banned him for you." Trish acted like she had done me a favor. I just nodded my head, walked to the kitchen, and poured me a cup of water. That bitch had me tired wrestling with her. Trish stood in the living room like she wanted me to come give her a hug or comfort her. Better yet, I'll give her some dick and treat her like a hoe like I should have from the beginning. No feelings involved this time. After I got my water, I went in the living room and grabbed Trish by her thighs, pulled her shorts off, and laid her on the floor. She said, "After all that, you want to have sex?" I ignored her and stuck my dick right in her. She closed her eyes and laid there. I didn't care. I was fucking her like I was just trying to catch my nut. I think she figured it out when I ejaculated on her face. I only did that to tell her, better yet, show her that she ain't shit. After I came all over Trish's face, I cleaned myself up and told her I'd be back. She went in the bathroom to clean her face. She didn't respond. I just left, thinking of my next move. Should I continue messing with Trish, or leave her alone? I know I said no feelings involved anymore but it was hard not thinking about her.

CHAPTER EIGHTEEN
"TOO MUCH DRAMA"

Me and Trish were not at our best. She was mad every day. Every single morning, she woke up angry. I couldn't hug her, even if I wanted. One afternoon, I took Trish and her kids to the library in Kissimmee, Florida. She was already tense and upset with whatever was on her mind. I asked Trish if she wanted to talk about it, she shook her head no. I didn't want to upset her, so I left it alone. As we walked out of the library, Trish asked me to give her a pen and paper. I passed the pen and paper to Justin to give to Trish. When Justin handed his mom the pen and paper, she got mad and said, "I asked you to get me the pen and paper, Vee. Why you gonna ask my son to give it to me?" I said, "Trish, what's wrong with you?" oh man, I shouldn't have said that. Trish opened the car door with a vengeance. She started yelling for Justin to get the fuck in the car. One look at her mom, and Gina didn't waste no time to run into the back seat.

Trish got in the front seat and slammed my car door. I

yelled, "Hey! What the fuck is wrong with you?" She yelled in a hot-tempered voice, "I asked you to do it, and you got my son to do the shit! I asked you! Not him!" I said, "Trish, what is the problem? You acting crazy in front of the kids, chill out." I couldn't believe she got mad for something so stupid. One minute into driving, Trish snapped. She started yelling as loud as she could. "You calling me crazy in front of my kids?" Out of nowhere, she punches me on the side of my face. What the fuck? What is wrong with Trish? I still didn't understand what was wrong with me giving Justin the pen and paper. She was trying to start a fight with me on purpose. Now I was pissed. I yelled, "Are you crazy? I'm driving! You gonna kill us all in this car!" Trish puts her back against the passenger car door, facing me and starts kicking me with all her might.

Honestly, I didn't understand what was causing her to be so violent. Whatever it was, it almost killed everyone in the car. I had to think of something quick because this bitch had seriously gone mad. If she kicks me in my face, she could knock me out and I would lose control of the steering wheel. It wasn't just my life she had no concern for, but her own kids' lives too. Trish cocked her foot back and kicked me on my arm. I ain't gon lie, that shit hurt like hell. With my right hand, I grabbed her ankle just when she cocked back to kick me again. I tightened my grip on her left ankle as she was trying to kick free. I held on as tight as I could but somehow, she got free. I tried to pull over, but there were ditches on both sides of the street and she was still kicking me with every fiber of her being. Finally, Trish cocked back for the last time, but before she could kick me again, I grabbed her ankle and pushed it. Her knee bent backward towards her face, hitting her on the lips. Immediately, Trish felt a sharp pain on her mouth. She stopped kicking me and sat up straight. Slowly, she moved her fingers up to her mouth touching her lips and saw blood.

Oh, my God, I thought. She's bleeding. The whole time this was going on, her kids sat down quietly and looked on like this was a TV show or something. Even after that crazy stunt she just pulled, trying to hurt me and all, I still asked, "Are you ok?" She wiped the blood from her mouth and just stared at it. The car was silent for what seemed like an eternity. Then suddenly, in a low tone, "Let... Me... Out...!" Knowing her, she was probably conjuring up a story about what happened to her lip. I pulled over on the side of the road and said, "Now you gonna tell people I hit you, huh?" She turned in my direction and made eye contact. Blood was dripping from her lips. She screamed at the top of her lungs, "I hate you!" She had said those exact words to me on more than one occasion, but I had never heard her say them with as much power as she had that day. It didn't feel right. I just couldn't wait to get away from her. Once again, I thought, I'm officially done with her. "That's okay," I replied. "Somebody loves me."

One of the things that would make her even more mad, was that I always had a slick comeback for every hurtful thing she said. I never let her see that the shit she said to me hurt me, just always had a slick remark. But honestly, what she said did hurt. And it cut deep. That's how I knew we were done. As I pulled over on the side of the road, she yelled, "Take me home!" I said, "Didn't you say pull over?" She yelled again, "Take me home!" I started driving once again. I didn't say a word to her. After driving for a couple minutes, I simply asked "Why?" She didn't respond. She just sat there looking mad. Her son, Justin, said out loud, "Mommy, why you hit Vee?" she turns to my direction, not even turning to face her son and yells, "Justin, why don't you mind your damn business!"

Justin started to cry. I said, "Don't cry Justin. Everything is ok, mommy's just playing." Trish says, "Oh, you think I'm playing?" Shaking my head, I said, "No Trish, I'm just telling him that, chill out!" She yells," pull over!" I said, "For what?" She says, "If you don't pull this bitch over, we all gonna die in this bitch together!" I took her threat seriously. The look in her eyes meant business. She had lost her mind. If she's crazy enough to kick me while driving, then this bitch is capable of doing anything stupid. I was trapped until I dropped her home or until she had a heart attack. I pulled over to a closed hardware store. She said, "Pull over to the back." I asked, "Why we going to the back?" She answered, "We gonna fight like niggas today!" Ok, at this point, I started laughing uncontrollably. She caught me off guard with her answer. Trish says, "Keep laughing bitch! Pull over right here."

Trish was serious. I pulled over and allowed her to get out the car but I was not gonna fight her. Yea, this bitch has definitely lost it. The car was still on. She got out of the passenger side and went behind the car, racing towards the driver side. I put the car on drive and drove off. I was going about 10-15 miles per hour. Trish was really tripping. She ran after the car like the terminator. I could see her through my rearview mirror. She was determined. If only she put all that energy into something positive. Now, I was going twenty miles per hour, but she was gaining up on me. I was kinda scared seriously. As Trish picked up speed, she tripped and fell, and started rolling. It was like a movie. This bitch is crazy, I thought. I stopped my car and reversed slowly. When I got close enough, Trish wasn't moving. She was laid out on her front side. The kids started asking me, "Vee, mommy fall down?" I told them, "I'm going to check and see if mommy is ok."

I put my car on park, took the keys out, and started walking to where Trish was laying. I was standing above her and called out her name, "Trish!" She made a slight noise, "Ahohhhh." I bent my knees to get on her level and make sure she was ok. She slowly started moving. I put my right hand on her head, and said, "Trish, get up." She was moving like a turtle, very slowly, but at least she was getting up. She was making noises like she was in a lot of pain. I'm sure she was but she was a bit over dramatic about it. I helped her up in fear that she might punch me while getting her up. I put her left arm around my neck, hoping she didn't try and put me in a head lock. I wrapped my right arm around her waist and helped her back to the passenger seat of my car. She started to tear up. Her cries were like that of a child. I wanted to say something, but every time I opened my mouth, she got furious. Trish's son, who seemed more concerned than her daughter, was asking questions like, "Mommy, are you ok?"

Trish sat quietly, touching her wounds. She had a bruise on her left leg above her knee. She just looked at her wounds and didn't say anything to anyone until she got home. Once we got to the apartment, I made sure the kids ate. Trish got out of the car and walked perfectly fine into the apartment. That night, she stayed in the bathroom for hours. Eventually, I decided to just leave. This was too much for me. I left without making a sound. I drove off heading to the burger place. After all this excitement, I was very hungry.

While eating, I get a picture text from Trish of the bruise on her leg. I texted her to put ice on it. I told her if that doesn't work, I'd take her to the hospital. She texted again, "Where are you?" I replied, "Getting something to eat." She asked, "Can you get me something to eat?" I was confused. Moments ago, she was trying to kill me and said she hated me, now she wants me to get her something eat? I'm not a doctor, but this bitch needs to be diagnosed with bipolar disorder or something.

I thought about it and thought about it. I just wanted to be done with her, but truth is, I still cared. I hated what I felt for her. It was like there was a spell over me that wouldn't let me leave her alone. I texted her back, "What would you like?" She replied, "A number one, medium, fruit punch, light on the ice." When I got back to her apartment, the kids were asleep in their room. I made sure they were asleep, not dead, especially after what she had pulled earlier. She was still in the bathroom.

She came out of the bathroom and sat next to me. She turned on a movie and started seducing me. Wait, what? Seducing me? After all that had just happened? What was going through Trish's head? She took all her clothes off and had on a red thong. After what happened, I couldn't get on hard. This is crazy, I thought. I didn't stop her because I figured if I did, she'd probably spaz out again. She massaged my dick until it got hard and sat on it. I came quick, as usual, hoping for whatever this was to end.

It has been several months since the incident. Me and Trish weren't the same anymore. Having sex with her was like fucking a dead corpse. She didn't move or moan. All she did was complain of her side hurting. Most of the time, she would stop every five minutes to get some water, purposely knowing I was almost ready to bust my nut. She had fell back into her way leaving the apartment dirty again. When the apartment was dirty, I'd leave and come back when it was clean. When Francis would go to work, I felt like I had an obligation to Trish's kids. I'd bring Maximus and Trish's kids to the park. Sometimes, Trish would come as well.

Francis would call to check up on Maximus and Trish would purposely make a lot of noise in the background so Francis would hear her. When Francis asked about who's that in the background? I'd tell her it was one of my hoes. She'd hang up. I knew she was pissed, but at least I wasn't lying. Francis texted me to keep my hoes away from her son and I'd text her back, "He's my son too."

Francis was upset with me and Trish would get closer to hear what me and Francis would talk about. I told Trish, "I'm not like you, you can listen anytime when me and Francis talk on the phone." Trish knew Francis stayed close, but she didn't know the exact address. After the park, I would drop Trish and her kids off. She'd ask, "Are you going to drop Maximus off?" "Yes, why?" I'd ask. She would always ask, "Why can't we come?" I was not going to show Trish where Francis stayed. Trish was an unstable ass woman that would start drama with Francis, and I could not have that on my chest. I lied to Trish and said I was going to pick Rob and his kids up, and there wouldn't be any room for her and the kids. One thing about Trish, she knew when I was lying, but she kept her mouth shut.

I was living a double life. You might as well call me a double agent. I was living with Francis and living with Trish and neither one of them said anything. My clothes were at Francis' house and I had a little bit of clothes in Trish's apartment. Most people would ask how I made that work. The answer would be, "Working two jobs and basically lying to both women." Sooner or later, I would have to make a choice though. Either I continue living this double life waiting for my lies to catch up with me or do the right thing and break it off with one of them.

I went to Francis' house. She had made it home from

work. She was asking Maximus who was he playing with and talking to? Maximus could talk a little now. He could say simple words and names. When Francis asked him who he was playing with, Maximus said, "Gina and Justin." I was shocked that Maximus said and pronounced their names right. Francis asked me, "Who is Gina and Justin?" Francis didn't know Trish's kids. I told Francis, "Why you asking me? Continue asking Maximus." She got upset and mumbled under her breath, "Keep your little secrets, that's fine." Even though me and Francis had our issues, I made sure she had everything she needed financially. I could see she wanted more though. She wanted me emotionally, mentally, and physically. She wanted my comfort. I was too tired from all the back and forth running around with Trish and working two jobs to give Francis what she needed.

I told Francis I was heading to work. By 4 PM, I had grabbed my uniform and placed it in my car. Francis said, "Aren't you forgetting something?" As she stood by the door way. I thought she wanted a hug from the expression on her face. I walked up towards her and placed my arms around her and gave her a hug. Francis yelled, "What are you doing?", and pushed me off her. I replied, "Isn't that what I forgot?" She responded, "You gets no love from me. Naw bruh. Just letting you know you forgot your ID." She yelled for Maximus to come to her. She said, "Maximus, tell daddy bye." Maximus said, "Bye", and Francis closed her door like she was done with me. I wasn't surprised she started to talk back now. All I could do was laugh about what Francis had just did. Oh well, it is what it is.

I then got into my car and headed back to Trish's apartment. Trish was in silent mode as always. She didn't say anything but mumbled under her breath. As soon as she saw me, she went straight into the shower. I thought to myself, "Why am I continuing what is not meant to be?" Clearly, me and Trish weren't happy together and her attitude was ugly. I was just tired and sick of whatever we had going on. Right now, was a better time than any other to end this relationship. While Trish was in the shower, I came in and said, "Trish, we need to talk." She didn't respond. She didn't say anything. I said, "Well, since you're not going to respond, I'm just gonna go ahead and say it." She pulled the shower curtain aside. She was standing there naked in the shower with the curtain pulled back. I said, "Trish, all we do is fight and argue. This isn't healthy for you or the kids. I love you. I really do, but I think we should just be friends."

Trish spoke. She said, "So you could go fuck them bitches on your Facebook page, huh? If I can't have you, I promise I will fuck your life up. You think it's a joke!!" I said, "Trish, you ain't want me in a while. All you do is play dead while we having sex. The way we used to feel about each other is gone. Now what I'll do for you and the kids is I'll still pay for the apartment until you get back on your feet or until your brother helps you with the rent, but I can't do it anymore." Her nose started flaring up. She was breathing heavier and heavier. She replied, "You're disgusting. All you think of is sex. You're disgusting." Trish paused and just let the water hit her body. Then, she turned to me slowly and said, "I'm pregnant."

CHAPTER NINETEEN
"A WOMAN SCORNED; VENGEANCE IS MINE"

Did Trish just say she was pregnant? It was like time had
stopped. I think I had stopped breathing for a slight moment.
In that split second, the only thought in my head was that
she was going to put me on child support and use the child
as a weapon to ruin my life. I almost fell on my knees and
prayed to God that this was all a joke. But then I thought to
myself, Trish is a compulsive liar. Worse than me, to be
honest. Besides, I already suspected her of messing with
someone else. I'd be a fool to believe that I was the only guy.
Trish was promiscuous. How could I trust someone like that
to tell me the truth? Maybe she's lying about the whole thing.
Maybe she's just saying that to keep me around. I said,
"Trish, you know what, I think you're lying." her eyes got
wider. Her face looked surprised. I thought to myself, this girl
will never leave me alone if I don't think of something quick.
A stupid idea came to mind, but I knew it might just work.
Why don't I just lie and tell her I found someone else?

It might not have been the best idea, but I gave it a shot. I said, "Trish, I've found someone new and I'm happy with her. What we had isn't working. The arguing and the fights. I don't think counseling would work. I'm sorry, I don't know what else to tell you." Trish's arms dropped to her side. Her head was down. She was about to explode, or so I thought. With her head still facing down, she mumbled, "Disgusting." I said, "What?" she replied, "You're a disgusting piece of shit. Go be with that bitch!" I don't know what came over me, but I started laughing. It didn't make things better. As a matter of fact, it made it worst. With a smirk on my face, I told Trish "I'ma go be with that bitch. At least she's a good woman." I could've easily let it go and let her get the last word, but I guess my pride wouldn't let me. Trish yelled, "Tell that bitch she ain't shit and you ain't shit! I'm glad I know what I know now, cause now I don't feel guilty." When she said that, I knew then that Trish was cheating. I just had never caught her. I figured, you know what, it's done. It's over. Let me just walk away. But no, I had to have the last word. "At least that bitch got a job!" I said.

Trish snapped. She jumped out the shower with lighting reflexes. Her wet body slid and she fell hard with a loud thump. That didn't stop her, it actually made her even more upset. All I saw was her naked and wet body running towards my direction. It was like a horror movie. I took off running, heading towards the apartment door. Trish took chase, still naked with her breast flapping up and down, side to side. There was water all over the floor of the apartment. My heart was beating fast. I ran towards the front door trying to unlock it quickly. Trish ran into the kitchen, grabbed a sharp knife, and ran quickly towards me. I finally unchained the door and managed to unlock it, but it was too late. Trish was seconds away from stabbing me. I had to think quick. I grabbed her laptop that was laid to my left and used it as a shield.

She swung the knife almost cutting me. Oh my God! She really was going to cut me. I didn't even want to know if she was going to kill me, so I pushed her back with the laptop. Trish fell on her back. I opened the door and ran outside. I must have been really out of shape because I was gasping for air hard. As I'm running towards my car, I look back and see Trish outside, but ass naked. She was screaming at me, "You don't think I'll come outside bitch! I don't give a fuck what these people think."

I finally made it to my car. It felt like I had just run a marathon. Once I got in, I started up my car. Oh shit! Trish jumped on top of the hood of my car, naked! Trish kept screaming, "Bitch ass nigga! Go be with your bitch!" She kicked the front window of my car, trying to break it. I reversed the car causing her crazy ass to almost fall on her face. Amazingly, Trish lands on her feet like a cat with her titties flapping and hitting her face. I then reversed all the way out the apartment complex. Trish ran after the car, still naked. This was very scary, but exciting. Don't judge me. Neighbors came out, not just for the drama, but to see Trish's naked body. She was used to letting people see her body, remember? She used to be a stripper. Only difference was, she wasn't getting paid for it this time. She had no shame. Her emotions must have blocked her embarrassment.

As soon as I reversed out of the apartment complex, I kept driving backwards until Trish stopped chasing the car. I could see her walking back to the apartment. The neighbors were outside watching and whistling. Some even took pictures. I felt this was truly the end between me and Trish. I wasn't coming back, no matter what. Now all my neighbors saw what happened. That was embarrassing. My cell phone was ringing uncontrollably. It was Trish calling. I said to myself, this time no matter what she does or says, I'm not going back to her. I answered. I know when I answer, I usually fall weak for Trish and go back to her. This time it was different. I knew it. She knew it. When I answered, she said, "Vee, I don't give a fuck what you do now, just give me my laptop." I said, "I don't have your laptop, you just trying to get me back. Well Trish, I'm not coming back." I then hung up.

I felt free, like a weight was lifted off my shoulder. She called back ten more times, leaving messages threatening to call the police. Damn, call the police? For what, I thought. This bitch finally lost her mind. After all I have done for her and her kids, would she? Would she really try to put me in jail? Trish hated the police anyways. After her arrest, I didn't think she would call them. On the eleventh call, I answered. She said, "I have the police here and they want to talk to you." I was shocked that Trish had the audacity to call the police on me. I was a little scared, but I said, "Ok, let me speak with the officer."

The officer introduced himself as Johnny. He said Trish is writing a report saying that you stole her laptop. I told the officer I didn't have her laptop and I would give him permission to search my car. He said, "Ok, can you come back down to the apartment?" I explained to the officer that I was heading to work. He said, "No problem," and asked if Trish's kids were mine. I told the officer that we had no children together, nor were we married. He said, "Ok, just try not to come back to her apartment." I said, "Yes officer." but let him know that the apartment she was staying in was under my name and I wanted her out. The officer pleaded, "But she has kids." I said, "Officer, this woman is trying to put me in jail, and you want me to feel sorry for her and her kids?" He replied, "Well, um, you'll have to do an official eviction." I told him I would.

After talking to the police, I thought I heard Trish tell the officer, "He also hit me." Then the phone hung up. Trish was trying her best to have me locked up. Was she that mad? I always figured she blamed me for her going to jail and she always wanted to make me feel her pain. She got even more upset when I made the comment about the other woman at least had a job. That was the icing on the cake that set everything off. The next day, I was at Francis' house. I felt free, liberated. I felt so much weight had been lifted off my shoulders. I decided to take Maximus and Francis out. To me, it was a celebration. To them, they were just happy to get out of the house and spend some time with me. I took them to Dave and Busters, Universal, and City Walk. The next three days were a fresh start for us, or so I thought. Trish didn't try to contact me, nor did I hear anything from her until I looked through my Facebook messages that night.

I had received numerous messages from various women on Facebook. Most of them had emailed me that Trish had contacted them, telling them vicious lies about me. She told one girl that me and Mason was talking about her and saying that she had sucked more dicks than Superhead. The other girl said Trish said that I had spread a rumor saying that she was promiscuous. There were several more emails coming in while I was still reading the first two. What the hell was Trish up to? She was on a mission, a dark path.

I remember Trish saying one afternoon, "If I can't have you, no bitch from North Miami gonna have you or ever want you. I promise I'll ruin your life if you leave me." I remember those words like they were yesterday. I guess she was keeping her promise. To me, Trish was thinking small. No girl from North Miami will want me? There's so many fish in the sea besides North Miami women. Why did she just think I only wanted to date North Miami women? Whatever the reason, Trish was contacting women I went to school with and spreading rumors. I figured she was trying to destroy my character. She wanted to play with fire. Ok, I'll give Trish a taste of her own medicine.

A while back Trish was being recorded from my iPod talking about certain people from high school. She knew she was being recorded because she looked and spoke right into the iPod video camera. Trish talked about this one girl who she thought was fake and called her a big hoe. Trish even talked about her male friend who didn't invite her to his wedding. He invited everyone from school, but her. Maybe his wife found out that he'd slept with Trish a couple of years back. I had found out through other people about them sleeping together. Eventually, she told me the truth.

She was so hurt about not being invited to the wedding, that she bashed her male friend and his new wife on the recording, calling them hypocrites. I said, "Fuck it!" Trish needed to be taught a lesson by her own hand. I decided to only send the recordings where she was talking about those people to each and every one of them. I didn't send the ones about her male friend though. I thought that might be going a little overboard. I uploaded the video and sent it to each of the girls that she had contacted about me too. I could've easily left Trish's crazy ass alone, but she was trying to destroy my character, who I was as a person. So, I gave her a taste of her own medicine.

A day later, as I was heading to work, my supervisor called me. He said, "Vee... Um, I'm gonna have to let you go." I asked, "Where?" Obviously, he was sending me to work at a different site. He said, "No Vee, I'm firing you." What the fuck? "Wait, what did I do to get fired?", I asked. He seemed as if he didn't want to tell me the real reason, but he ended up telling me. He said a woman had called, and said that I was stealing gas. She also told him that I had been stealing other items from the property. He said that she even went into details of the security office and where the gas cards were located. I said, "Wait, how can you just believe a random person? I've been there for years." He said, "She claims to be your girlfriend. She even came up here Vee. It's just too many problems for this company. Sorry, but we can't afford to lose our contract."

I was devastated. How could this bitch go this far and cause me to lose my job? I was so mad that I wanted to go over there and burn that apartment down. It was the center of evil and it needed to be cleansed. I told my supervisor that's fucked up and told him to kiss my black ass. I didn't like him anyways. Him nor the property managers. They all seemed like Klan members anyway, shaved bald heads and all from Texas! They couldn't fool me. I hung the phone up on my supervisor. I pulled over because now, I didn't have a job to go to. Trish was trying to hurt me by stopping my money flow too. So now she planned to fuck me over by calling my job? Even after all I had done for Trish and her kids, this is how she repays me. I didn't know what I was going to tell Francis about me losing my job. The only thing I could think of was to look for another job while I was driving about.

Not even four hours had passed, I received a call from a juvenile correctional facility in orange county Florida. They asked me if I could come in for an interview? I was excited, almost lost for words. I said, "Yes, I'll definitely be there tomorrow at 9 AM." I was happy, filled with bliss. Nothing could ruin my day now. As I was driving home, I received a phone call from Mason. The first words from Mason were, "You see? I told you she was going to try and fuck your life up." I was confused. I hadn't even told Mason what was going on yet. He said, "Vee, have you not been on Facebook?" I said, "No, why?" He said Trish was on Facebook blasting me. She was telling people that I had abused her. At first, I was shocked, flabbergasted. Apparently, she even put my picture up on social media saying that I forced her to move to central Florida. The worst part was that she said that I forced her to have sex with me and forced her to suck my dick. Oh my God! This was unbelievable.

Trish had sunk to a new low. Was she that upset that she would take it to a new level of destroying my character? I couldn't breathe. "Mason, are you serious?", I asked. He said, "Vee, I don't want to say I told you so, but I did. She even has followers telling her to call the police on you." "But I didn't even do any of those things she's accusing me of," I told Mason. He said he figured that because he knows me. "Besides," he says. "What woman would post up pictures and discuss a situation like this on Facebook? One that is not right in the head." I agreed with Mason, but I really wanted to see what pictures she had posted. I drove off to Francis' house. It took about fifteen minutes to get home from where I was.

I was with Mason on the phone the whole time. When I got to Francis' house, she was not home yet and Maximus was still in day care. I went straight to the desktop in Francis' computer room. Immediately, I logged on to Facebook. I had forgotten that I had blocked Trish's Facebook a while back when we were arguing. I couldn't see her page! By now

I'm stressed and kinda freaking out. Mason gave me his Facebook password so I could log in. He said, "I want you to see it while I'm on the phone with you Vee." Once I logged on with Mason's info, I went on Trish's pages. She had pictures of me and her together. She was telling people that she had been dating me for over two years and how I have been hiding her from the world. She even said I kept her from her family and friends.

I looked at the other pictures that she had posted. She put pictures up of the bruises she had received from when she was kicking me in the car a while back. She also put up the bruises from when she had fallen from chasing the car. She posted the pictures with the caption, "Look at the bruises he has caused me." I thought, oh my God! This bitch is really trying to damage my reputation. There were so many comments under the photos. People commented saying things that really upset me. Most of the people who commented were people that I'd known for years. They just judged me in a split second without me telling my side of the story. Some were like, "He's an animal." "Leave him." "He will do it again." "Come stay with me, he knows a lot of people in Miami." A few of them even said, "You need to lock him up girl!" "No woman deserves to be abused."

Most of the followers, I noticed, were people who weren't levelheaded anyway. Many of them were simple minded people who'd only heard one side of the story. Others were victims of domestic violence themselves and made their judgements because I was a big man who had a history of fighting back in high school. This is exactly what Trish wanted. Divide and conquer. To my surprise, there was one woman who seemed to be Trish's spokesperson. She was a woman from my past. One that I'd had a sexual relationship with and things didn't end well. Her name was Zeena

Michaels.

Zeena was a woman who was no more than a sex buddy. I had met her six months before I had met Trish. Zeena was a few years older than me and had two little boys. She didn't work. She was a divorced woman, living across an apartment from the father of her children. An apartment where he and his new girlfriend were living in. It was a sick situation, but like I said, she was just a fuck buddy. Zeena was living off her son's disability check. I had met her in college. She was very persuasive when she first stepped up to me. She was short, thick, had huge breasts, a flat butt, and had a way of talking. She was always licking her lips seductively. It was her personality that caught my attention, and her vulgar comments that sunk me in. Zeena always would lure me in with sex. She talked about how she'd sucked the juices out of my nut sacks, that shit was sexy. She got me with that and from then on, I went to her apartment every other day just to get some head.

Zeena was a smoker so we never kissed. I hated the smell and taste of cigarettes. One day at Zeena's apartment, I found a dildo that was the size of my arm. Zeena gave good filacio, but to be honest, she didn't have any walls to hit. Meaning her pussy was as wide as a cave and my dick was like an ant trying to fit in. This wasn't going to work between me and her. I disappeared after a few weeks of fucking and getting my dick sucked from Zeena. Zeena went around school looking for me. She even left messages on my cell phone saying her and her kids needed my help. Fuck them, they're not my kids. I know that sounds bad, but that's how I was feeling. Don't use your kids for me to help you and plus, Zeena told me stories of her sleeping with married men. Did she really think that we were going to be a couple after those stories? And not to mention that big ass dildo?

Hell naw!

Come to find out, Trish and Zeena had known each other for a long time. A few months back, I found out Zeena had contacted Trish asking her about me on Facebook. She was saying things like, "Oh girl, I didn't know you were dating Vee?" "I didn't even know you knew him." Trish had asked me about Zeena months ago, and I told her the truth. Zeena was just a booty call. Trish used that info to her advantage. She was able to pull Zeena in on the attack on Facebook. Zeena was Trish's general on all the negative posts about me. Zeena was commenting on every single pic, adding fuel to the fire. She was saying things like, "His little dick, insecure ass man." Clearly, these two women were bitter and they both had one thing in common, revenge.

I decided, man, fuck them bitches! I'm not going to respond, I'll just ignore it. This was clearly cyber bullying. Zeena contacted me on Facebook calling me every kind of name there was in the book. I didn't curse her out or call her names, which I could have. But I did the one thing I don't think she nor I expected. I apologized to Zeena for disappearing on her and said, "If you're mad at me for disappearing, let me just say, I apologize. You can call me any name you want. I'm not going to argue with you." Zeena wanted a negative reaction from me. I wasn't going to give it to her. Hell, I shoulda never responded to her email message. Even then, she continued to blast me and use the name of God to wish me hell. I told her thank you and have a nice day. Her last email said, "Bitch ass." That showed just how immature she still was. There was no reasoning with someone like that, she was bitter.

I told Mason about it. He said, "Vee, I feel something bad is going to happen, so keep your guards up." I was mad, but I was not going to respond or react to any of Trish's status updates on Facebook. I never believed in cyber bullying before this. I always figured that you could just turn the computer off and it would all go away, but that isn't the case. This was getting stressful. I told Mason I'll call him tomorrow. With all this drama, I just needed to be at peace.

The next day Francis was off. She decided to keep Maximus with her instead of sending him to day care. Francis saw me on the couch and said, "You don't look so good. Is everything alright?" I told her that I was let go from my job. She burst out in shock, "What happened Vee?" I told her, "Don't worry, I found another job." Francis wanted to know what happened, but I couldn't tell her that Trish, my side chick, got me fired. I told Francis they were cutting back and letting people go. I hated to lie about that, but what else was I going to say? I told Francis that I had an interview this morning and that everything was working out for the best. Francis said she wanted to go with me to the interview with Maximus. That was fine with me, so I told her to get ready. I was stressing about everything that was going on, but I couldn't let Francis see that.

Francis had gotten Maximus ready and now she was ready. I decided to drive Francis' car to the interview. I figured after the interview, we could all go get breakfast. I was well dressed. White button down long sleeved shirt and black dress pants. It took us twenty-five minutes to get to the juvenile facility. I was ready for this interview. When I walked into the interview, I felt it would be a piece of cake. There were two people asking me twenty questions and I did great answering all of them. At the end, they asked, "When can you start? " I told them, "Right away." They said, "We'll start you tomorrow." I walked out of that interview like a champion. I got in the car with Francis and Maximus and drove off excited. When I told Francis the news, she was so happy. I said, "Let's go to Bennigans." Maximus started singing his alphabet song and it was the cutest moment. A very happy moment.

As I was driving, a police officer pulled up behind me and started flashing his lights. I pulled over onto the side of the road and turned off the car. The officer came to my window and said, "License and registration please." I gave him my license and Francis' registration. He walked back to his car and stayed there for more than ten minutes. After about ten minutes, another police car pulled up behind the first cop's car. Something wasn't right. My heart was beating fast. Francis said, "Well, this don't look good." Maximus said, "Daddy, what police doing?" I told him they're eating donuts." He laughed and said, "No they're not."

I could see two police officers (one white and one black) walking towards my car. When they got to my side of the door, they said, "Step out the car please." I asked is everything ok officers?" the white cop seemed more aggressive and yelled, "Step out the car now!" in a forceful tone. I was getting scared. Now he wants me to get out of the car? I got out the car. The white cop said, "Turn around!" I turned around like he said. Now I was really scared. I didn't want to give this cop a reason to shoot me. He grabs my hand forcefully and slaps handcuffs on my wrists. Francis yells, "What's going on?!" Maximus yells, "Let my daddy go! Bad police! You no good." My heart is hurting. Why is this going on? I've never been arrested and here this white officer is being very nasty as if he wants to taze me. Yelling and telling me to make a move and I'm spraying your ass! What the hell is going on?

The other officer seemed more reasonable. They both

walked me to the police car. Each one holding each one of my arms. They were treating me like a criminal. Once they put me in the police car, I could hear Francis crying so loudly. It was painful to hear. I hear my son, Maximus saying, "Don't cry mommy." I just wanted to die. I said to the reasonable officer, "Why am I being arrested, is this a joke?" he said, "No sir, I can assure you that this is not a joke." He looked in his computer and asked, "Do you know a Trisha Nelson?" My face dropped. He said, "Well, you're being arrested for domestic violence." Oh my God, this is exactly what Trish wanted. Why didn't I listen to Mason and everyone that said not to mess with her? Damn, something is truly wrong with her. Not even her own family messes with her.

I couldn't believe this. I was being arrested. How could this happen? Trish must have used the pictures from her past bruises and said I did that to her. Why would she lie? Did she really want to see me destroyed? This was crazy. I don't deserve to be arrested. This was not fair. The shame, the pain, the embarrassment to my family while my son watched. I felt like less than a man for my son to see me in handcuffs. And Francis, her tears brought pain to my heart. This wasn't supposed to happen like this. Why didn't I listen? I should have listened to the warnings.

As the cop is about to drive off, I look back at Francis and Maximus. My heart is so heavy. I feel like I can't breathe. Francis' cries while holding Maximus on her left shoulder. As the cop drove off with me, I hear Maximus say, "Mommy, don't cry", and wipes her tears away. All I could think about is how I didn't mean to hurt you, Francis and Maximus. I was selfish. I only thought about my needs and my pleasures. I only thought about myself. That's all I could think of as a tear fell from my eye. As reality sunk in, I tell myself to close my eyes and open them because this was just a bad dream. But I can't wake up because it's a nightmare that has taken the form of reality. I blame myself. I blame myself for not listening. I blame myself for not stopping it where it began. I blame myself for having a mistress. Now I'm feeling the vengeance and the consequence of a sidechick.

ABOUT THE AUTHOR

Vladimir Dubois, a Haitian American writer, was born on May 5, 1981 in Miami, Florida. Throughout the years, he excelled in fine arts. As a child, Vladimir won various awards for his artwork and later, became an impressive singer/songwriter. As a young adult, Vladimir began competing in weight lifting competitions and even won two 1st place trophies for bench pressing. Vladimir has had an interesting life, and in his first book, Consequences of a SideChick, he exposes many of those life situations. Adding to his list of many creative talents, Vladimir has now written the sequel to this book, Consequences of a SideChick 2: Fool Me Twice, Shame on Me and also written and directed his first and second plays, Consequences of a SideChick: The Play part 1 and part 2. Expect more from Vladimir because the best is yet to come.

Made in the USA
Columbia, SC
17 February 2022

55860749R00114